Praise for Robert Mulindwa's first book, *Created for Success*

Wow! Scriptural, Inspiring, Sobering. This is packed with motivation. And scriptural motivation! It's all about living life to the fullest with the time we have here, which is precious.

If only I'd read this sooner!

Well I can tell you, this author is living his purpose, and I am so thankful I've caught a glimpse! This work has awakened God's calling within me!

Get the book!

—F. Marie

5 out of 5 stars, must read!

Created For Success is an uplifting and inspiring book that will appeal to anyone who wants to find meaning and purpose in life. Whether you are a person of faith or just someone looking to find your way, this book offers practical tools and insights that will help you achieve your goals.

Highly recommended!

—Jake Jeffery Ward

Such a great book!

This book is a compelling and insightful guide for individuals seeking to align their lives with their divine purpose. It will remind us that a meaningful life is one guided by faith, purpose, and love..

—Van V

Insightful Read!

In an era where the measure of success is often based on comparative achievements and external impressions, this enlightening book posits that real, authentic success comes from discovering our purpose in life. It underscores the idea that true fulfillment and contentment stem from realizing and living out this unique purpose.

The book serves as a guide, leading readers on a journey of self-discovery and introspection, urging them to look within themselves for their intrinsic value and potential.

With the guidance of the Holy Spirit, as the book suggests, we can align our inner selves with our outer lives, creating a harmonious existence filled with success that is genuine and deeply satisfying.

This book is not merely a good read; it's a transformative experience that challenges conventional notions of success and beckons readers to seek a deeper, more meaningful kind of achievement.

—Charles C

REDISCOVERING IDENTITY

Books by Robert Mulindwa

Created for Success

Rediscovering Identity

REDISCOVERING IDENTITY

You

Are

The

Image

Of

God.

ROBERT MULINDWA

KINGDOM COME

PUBLISHING

KINGDOM COME

PUBLISHING

Copyright © 2023 by Robert Mulwinda
All rights reserved.
Published by Kingdom Come Publishing
Nashville, TN

No part of this book may be reproduced in any manner without written permission except in the case of brief quotations embodied in critical articles and reviews.

For information about special discounts for bulk purchases or **author interviews, appearances, and speaking engagements** please contact:

www.RobertMulindwa.com
MulindwaRobert123@gmail.com

First Edition

ISBNs
ISBN Hardcover   979-8-9876653-3-6
ISBN Paperback   979-8-9876653-4-3
ISBN Ebook   979-8-9876653-5-0

Library of Congress: 2023920906

Edited, cover, book and page design by Rodney Miles www.RodneyMiles.com
Crown image used in cover by Alana Jordan from Pixabay

The image of God in humanity is not a static possession, but a dynamic invitation to reflect His character, love, and creativity in the world

— Unknown

To the memory of my mom,
Bena Nakafero
1952-2021

Preface

SINCE THE DAWN of time, the notion of human identity has been a subject of discussion across various cultures and civilizations. Along the continuum of time, it has attracted the attention of philosophers, psychologists, sociologists, theologians, ad infinitum. However, in the grand scheme of things human identity cannot be understood without addressing human origin. And you can't talk about human origin without mentioning the origin of the Earth or the universe.

Now, in an attempt to address this relevant and significant conundrum relating to human identity, human origin, and the beginning of time, theories like the Big Bang as well as the theory of evolution penetrate my mind. Scientists claim to comprehend the first moments and evolution of our universe, but areas of uncertainty persist. Enter the Big Bang, which was a rapid change of a tiny point of matter into a vast and expanding universe. This tiny point of matter is referred to as a *singularity*[1] and was proposed by Georges Lemaître[2]. Over millions of years coupled with randomness, the energy cooled into particles of matter. It's this matter that is the origin of animate and inanimate creatures in the universe. This presents a drawback as to *what brought about the singularity* that metamorphosed into the Big Bang. Which begs the question; "Prior to the Big Bang what existed?"

Delving deeper into this crusade and pilgrimage, Charles Darwin[3] continued on a journey of evolutionary theory that was initiated by his grandfather Erasmus Darwin. In his *theory of evolution by natural selection*, Charles Darwin contends that organisms better suited to their environment are able to reproduce more

---

[1] Put simply, singularities are places where the mathematics "misbehave," typically by generating infinitely large values. — https://www.livescience.com/what-is-singularity

[2] https://www.amnh.org/learn-teach/curriculum-collections/cosmic-horizons-book/georges-lemaitre-big-bang

[3] English naturalist whose scientific theory of evolution by natural selection became the foundation of modern evolutionary studies. — https://www.britannica.com/biography/Charles-Darwin

successfully. And this was referred to as *survival of the fittest*. Not in the sense of physical strength, but in the ability to survive and reproduce. Later on fellow scientists challenged Darwin because the theory couldn't validate how new species would emerge out of existing ones. Darwin lacked knowledge on the mechanism of *inheritance*[4], and offered no suitable explanation on the source of genetic information.

As I journey further into this subject matter, important to note is that both theories of the Big Bang and evolution, like many other scientific theories that attempt to explain the triad of human identity, human origin, and beginning of time, are shrouded in a blanket of drawbacks. A common theory of evolution asserts that mankind developed from apelike mammals. A *species* refers to a group of the same kind that is able to reproduce according to its kind over and again. One thing to note is that a variety does exist within a specie. For instance, there are a variety of cows, and propagating among them will always yield a

---

[4] Inheritance refers to the transmission of traits or information from one generation of individuals or cells to the next. — https://www.sciencedirect.com/topics/biochemistry-genetics-and-molecular-biology/inheritance

cow. There's no evidence of continual propagation between different species. I have never seen a half cow and half goat as one creature. Implying that there's no way a cow over periods of years evolved from anything else other than a cow. Similarly, science can't validate how a human being evolved from anything that is not human.

A friend of mine happens to own a farm with different species of animals. Among them are horses, mules, and donkeys. One day she pointed out an interesting fact that a mule is a product of propagation between a horse and a donkey. However, the mule cannot propagate. That is, it lacks the ability to reproduce. Why? Because continual propagation is only possible between the same species.

Matters of divinity cannot simply be explained away by science. More findings from science present more questions than answers. However, for every human creation or product we are quick to acknowledge the intelligence and purpose behind it, including the manufacturer. This kind of thinking should parallel the idea that this great universe and everything in it including mankind, is the handiwork of the Almighty Devine, the most intelligent of designers who is purposeful.

*In the beginning
God created the heavens
and earth.*

Genesis 1:1

By decree and command, the Lord God spoke things into existence. "Let there be… " and it was so. And God saw that it was good. This brought into existence the moon, sun, stars, birds, fish, vegetation, and animals. The birds, fish, animals, and vegetation were created after their kind. However, when it came to man God turned to Himself and said:

*Let us make mankind
in our image and likeness.*

Genesis 1:26

May the Spirit of God enlighten our eyes of understanding as we traverse this rational, conceptual, and spiritual excursion in discerning the idea that human identity is the image of God.

Let God be true
and every human being a liar.

Romans 3:4

Robert Mulindwa
Nashville, Tennessee
October, 2023

Contents

Praise for Robert Mulindwa's first book,
Created for Success i

Preface ix

Contents xv

Introduction 1

[1]   Knowing God & Discovering Self 7

[2]   Tranquility in Eden, Then the Temptation 25

[3]   Humankind's Enduring Image & Likeness
of God Beyond the Fall 45

[4]   Shadows of Humankind's Redemption 61

[5]   In Redemption, the Past is Forgiven,
and the Future is Salvaged 79

[6]   Beloved of Christ, the Devil is a Liar 97

[7]   Jesus Christ as the Flawless & Exemplary
Image of God's Nature 115

[8] The Interplay Between Culture & Identity . 137

[9] Espousing the Truth of Who God Says You Are 151

[10] Central to True Identity is the Transformation from Slaves to Sons 169

Conclusion 187

About the Author 195

Thank You 197

You Were Created for Success! 199

Notes 201

"Every human being, regardless of their circumstance or station in life, possesses an inherent dignity and worth because they bear the image of God."

— Pope Francis

Introduction

I HAPPENED TO come across an account of a 33-year-old Frenchman who goes by the pseudonym, "Black Alien[5]." So as to live up to his name, he has undergone several body transformations. This extraterrestrial wishful thinker had his nose and upper lip cut off. Next was the splitting of his tongue, I guess to have a fork-like appearance. As if that was not enough, he had his entire body covered in tattoos. To say that his appearance is grotesque is an understatement. His latest body alteration involved the cutting off of two fingers from his left hand, in a bid to have a claw-like appearance.

---

[5] https://nypost.com/2023/01/24/i-modified-my-body-to-be-a-black-alien-now-restaurants-are-scared-to-serve-me/

REDISCOVERING IDENTITY

Anthony Loffredo, aka "Black Alien," is not done yet. Even with these disturbing body mutilations and alterations, he made it known that only 34 percent of his ambition to become an alien has been achieved. Obviously, he has a massive social media following, but in real life he suffers from social stigma due to his looks. Now, a psychologist or psychiatrist would certainly assign him one or more diagnoses listed in the *Diagnostic and Statistical Manual of Mental Disorders (DSM)*, however, this may not address the root cause of this odd behavior.

Why?

I believe his actual problem is a detachment from his Source which presents an identity problem. Like many people, the Black Alien is suffering from ignorance of the fact that he is created in the image of God. The starting point in remedying this problem is to seek the knowledge, understanding, and wisdom of God.

Introduction

This reminds me of an encounter between German philosopher Arthur Schopenhauer[6] and a policeman. Schopenhauer might have been mistaken for a beggar or wanderer due to his dressing style. It so happened 100 years ago as he sat on a park bench in deep contemplation, that he drew the attention of a policeman. In answering the call of duty, the policeman proceeded to ask the philosopher, "Who are you?"

His response was, "I would to God I knew."

The only truth about who we are is in God. This parallels a New Testament account question by Jesus Christ to his disciples:

"Who do people say I am?"

In unison they answered, "Some say John the Baptist, others say Elijah, and others one of the prophets."

---

[6] Arthur Schopenhauer was a German philosopher born on 22 February 1788 in Danzig. He is best known for his 1818 work, The World as Will and Representation, which characterizes the phenomenal world as the manifestation of a blind and irrational noumenal (an object that exists independently of human sense) will. —https://en.wikipedia.org/wiki/Arthur_Schopenhauer

"But what about you?" he asked. "Who do you say I am?"

Peter answered, "You are the Messiah, the Son of the Living God."[7]

Interesting and important to note is the response that Jesus gave Peter. He refused to give him credit, much as Peter's response was spot on. Instead, Jesus clearly acknowledged that only through revelation from God, Peter was able to respond correctly. Jesus is saying Peter as a human does not have the capacity to discern Jesus' true identity. Only with the help of the Spirit of God can Peter get revelation.

Intuitively, no human has the ability to know and understand the identity of another human. Correspondingly, no human can understand the truth about his or her own identity without revelation from God. This is a reminder of our divine origin, affirming that we are in God's image with inherent value and worth, regardless of our circumstances.

---

[7] Mathew 16:13-17

Introduction

In this book, we will explore this fundamental question about humanity, a profound issue that has intrigued us for ages. That question is, "Who am I?" To do this, we will turn to the timeless wisdom and guidance that can only be found in the sacred texts of the Bible, because we have been provided answers there.

REDISCOVERING IDENTITY

[1]

Knowing God & Discovering Self

True knowledge of God is inseparable from true knowledge of oneself, for in seeking God, we discover the deepest truths about who we are and our purpose in this magnificent universe.

— Unknown

IN HIS FINAL book, Stephen Hawking suggests the likelihood of the existence of God in our universe is one to be multiplied by zero. His view of creation was premised on a scientific perspective. His response to the most burning questions of our time—"Where do we come from?" and "What is our purpose?"—was "I think the universe was spontaneously created out of nothing, according to the laws of science." This gentleman also at one point asserted, "If you accept as I do, that the laws of nature are fixed, then it doesn't take long to ask: What role is there for God?" You wouldn't be surprised to know that Hawking was an avid proponent of the Big Bang Theory.

As I mentioned earlier, the Big Bang Theory is predicated on the idea that the universe began by exploding suddenly out of an ultra-dense singularity smaller than an atom. In his attempt to validate the Big Bang, Hawking postulated, "We have finally found something that doesn't have a cause because there was no time for a cause to exist in." Not to be outdone, he further claimed, "For me this means that there is no possibility of a creator, because there is no time for a creator to have existed in."

Like many scientists, Hawking premised his argument on the tried and tired premise of *randomness* as a precursor to the birth of the

[1] Knowing God & Discovering Self

universe and everything in it. So, another drawback to his assertions is the absence of the concept of time prior to the Big Bang.

To postulate that the universe came into existence by some scenario predicated on randomness is to affirm that chance is the reason Earth exists. This is to further suggest that as humankind we are a product of chance. Randomness as a hallmark of our existence relegates us to being champions of haphazardness lacking definite aim. This parallels the idea of flipping a coin or tossing of a dice, or even playing Russian roulette[8].

A closer look at Hawking's suggestion of zero existence of time prior to the Big Bang implies no presence of a creator because there was no time to exist in. This demonstrates his lack of insight in relation to the eternal God. The God who created the universe and everything in it resides in eternity. Eternity is a time without measure. The eternal God

---

[8] Lethal game of chance in which a player places a single round in a revolver, spins the cylinder, places the muzzle against a person and pulls the trigger. —https://en.wikipedia.org/wiki/Russian_roulette

does not live in the concept of time and doesn't require one.

To have *insight* requires a deeper comprehension of God. Our understanding of God paves the way for our own self-discovery. Scriptural enlightenment is the roadmap to discerning the true essence and nature of God. The existence of creation validates the existence of God. *Scripture in its entirety is inspired by the Spirit of God.*

All Scripture is God-breathed and is useful for teaching, rebuking, correcting, and training in righteousness, so that the servant of God may be thoroughly equipped for every good work.

2 Timothy 3:16-17

The apostle Paul corroborates in Romans:

[1] Knowing God & Discovering Self

*For since the creation of the world
God's invisible qualities—his
eternal power and divine nature—
have been clearly seen, being
understood from what has been
made so that people are
without excuse.*

Romans 1:20

This clearly illustrates that the hallmarks of God's creation are *purposefulness* and *intelligence*. In all of God's creation mankind is in a class all by himself.

Why?

On the sixth day of creation, God reached into His inner core and said:

REDISCOVERING IDENTITY

Let us make mankind in our image, after our likeness: and let them have dominion over the fish of the sea, and over the fowl of the air, and over the cattle, and over all the earth, and over every creeping thing that creeps on land.

Genesis 1:26

Now, let's embark on a journey to unpack this exceptional, noteworthy, and momentous verse. Believing is first necessary, as it leads to revelation. First, let me consider what the essence of God's image is about. It refers to the nature and character of God. "Image of God" has nothing to do with *appearance* because God has no physical form. This is corroborated by Paul the Apostle:

[1] Knowing God & Discovering Self

Now the Lord is the Spirit and where the Spirit of the Lord is, there is freedom.

2 Corinthians 3:17

Therefore, only when mankind understands that he is the image of God can he know himself.

However, comprehension of the image is only possible with fully understanding the object. Intuitively, for mankind to fully grasp his identity, knowledge of God is a must. The Bible describes God as:

- Omnipotent
- Omniscient
- Omnipresent
- Omnibenevolent
- Transcendent
- Eternal
- Immanent
- Creator

- Holy
- Just
- Indelible
- *ad infinitum.*

Truth of the matter is God is indescribable. All we know is what He chooses to reveal to us. His thoughts are not our thoughts, and His ways are not our ways.

> *"For my thoughts are not your thoughts, neither are your ways my ways," declares the Lord. "As the heavens are higher than the earth, so are my ways higher than your ways and my thoughts than your thoughts."*
>
> Isaiah 55:8-9

As omnipotent, God possesses unlimited power, and He is all-powerful. As omniscient, God is

[1] Knowing God & Discovering Self

infinitely knowing. Being able to be present in all places at the same time is what makes God omnipresent. God is superior or supreme in excellence, therefore transcendent. Without beginning or end to His existence makes God eternal. When it comes to all His attributes or characteristics that define His nature, God can exist all by Himself and still be fulfilled.

Or, can He?

God is benevolent, that is, He has a disposition to do good, possessing love to mankind and a desire to promote humankind's prosperity and happiness. Apostle John authenticates this:

And so we know and rely on the love God has for us. God is love. Whoever lives in love lives in God, and God in them.

1 John 4:16

Hence, *God is love*. God doesn't show love, He *is* love. It is only in this disposition that the Almighty can't exist all by Himself and still be fulfilled. It's for this reason the economy of God as the Trinity decides to create a creature with similar essence. Notice I said "similar," not "the same" because humankind is not wholly identical and equal to God, however humankind to some degree bears the essence of God. I can therefore state unequivocally the primary reason for creating mankind as the image of God was *so that man could fellowship with God*. For love to be experienced, it must be shared through fellowship and companionship.

Note that *fellowship with God* and *rulership of the nonhuman creation* are crucial in the manifestation of God's image. The dominion mandate uniquely places man above all His creation. There exists a great gulf between man and animals. Anatomically and physiologically there are some shared similarities, but man exhibits rationality, morality, and spirituality. When you look at Genesis 1:26, man was created fully-grown and developed.

[1] Knowing God & Discovering Self

Then God said, "Let us make mankind in our image, in our likeness, so that they may rule over the fish in the sea and the birds in the sky, over the livestock and all the wild animals, and over all the creatures that move along the ground."

Genesis 1:26

This counters the idea put forward by science that man is the product of evolution that occurred over millions of years ago, and that this was simply premised on chance. Evolution insinuates that man originated from lower forms of life that developed into apes from which man emerged. Like I pointed out earlier, "Let God be true and every man a liar." (Romans 3:4)

The gulf between man and animals can never be bridged because for dominion on behalf of God to be carried out, *man must rule* over nonhuman creation. It's having the image and likeness of God that makes dominion possible. Likeness requires functioning like God.

> *So God created humanity in his image, in the image of God He created him, male and female He created them.*
>
> *Genesis 1:27*

In his book, *The Liberating Image—The Imago Dei in Genesis 1*, J. Richard Middleton articulates:

[1] Knowing God & Discovering Self

> *On the one hand, careful exegesis of Genesis 1:26-28, in conjunction with an intertextual reading of the symbolic world of Genesis 1, does indeed suggest that the imago Dei refers to human rule, that is, the exercise of power on God's behalf in creation... said one way, humans are like God in exercising royal power on earth. Said another way, the divine ruler delegated to humans a share in his rule of the earth.*

In carrying out the rulership mandate, humankind serves as a representative of God on Earth. In fact, Middleton expounds that:

> *... the delegation of or sharing in, God's rule suggests the image as representative, designating the responsible office and task entrusted to humanity in administering the earthly realm on God's behalf.*

Now, as bearers of God's image humankind has inherent value and worthiness. Even when mankind denies God or disobeys God, still he is a bearer of God's image. However, when you believe in the existence of God as well as fully understanding that you are an image of God, it creates a boundary within which you live your life. There are values, beliefs, and standards to which you hold yourself accountable.

It doesn't matter what your family background is, you are an image of God. It doesn't matter the color of your skin or race, you are an image of God. People's opinions of you, be it friends, teachers, parents, or spouse don't matter. When you fully grasp the essence of being created in God's image,

[1] Knowing God & Discovering Self

even your weaknesses don't negatively impact your identity. Why? Because the Bible says:

> *My grace is sufficient for you, for
> my power is made perfect
> in weakness.*
>
> *2 Corinthians 12:9*

Thoroughly understanding that your true identity is the image of God makes it impossible for anyone to try to ascribe any description contrary to this, and you believe them. Remember that the last thing the devil wants is an individual who without a doubt knows their identity in God. And it's shameful and tragic for any living individual to not know who they are.

The great Apostle Paul says:

REDISCOVERING IDENTITY

For our struggle is not against flesh and blood, but against the rulers, against the authorities, against the powers of this dark world and against the spiritual forces of evil in the heavenly realms.

Ephesians 6:12

Paul is implying the devil operates round the clock to confuse innocent and unsuspecting individuals by distorting their view of who they are. For instance, negative opinions about you from an associate. Irrespective of what the devil does, always remember that you are who God says you are:

[1] Knowing God & Discovering Self

For you created my inmost being, you knit me together in my mother's womb. I praise you because I am fearfully and wonderfully made, your works are wonderful, I know that full well. My frame was not hidden from you when I was made in the secret place, when I was woven together in the depths of the earth. Your eyes saw my unformed body; all the days ordained for me were written in your book before one of them came to be.

Psalms 139:13-16

This should get you feeling exceptional, extra special, and significant, because you are. From this verse we infer that God was so very careful as He made you and me. He filled us with wonder, in that He is awestruck by His own creation. You are so important that as soon as you were conceived in

REDISCOVERING IDENTITY

your mother's womb, He never took His eyes off of you. Did you know that each one of us has a book of life already written out and complete before we even start in the physical world? This says God completed you and me in the spiritual realm, before He manifested us in the physical realm.

Your life is not an experiment, your identity is already predestined by God.

[2]

Tranquility in Eden, Then the Temptation

Before the fall, man stood in perfect harmony, a reflection of the divine image, radiating innocence, wisdom, and a boundless capacity to love and create.

— *Unknown*

STUDYING SCRIPTURE REVEALS that Genesis 1 is a prologue in relation to creation, and Genesis 2 the detailed account. Close observation indicates that after the creation of the heavens and Earth in Genesis 1, what follows can be defined as chaos and confusion. Moses, the law giver asserted:

And the earth was without form and void; and darkness was upon the face of the deep. And the Spirit of God moved upon the face of the waters.

Genesis 1:2

This verse describes a situation that is out of control, and out of order which in no way defines the nature or essence of God. *Elohim*[9] is the God of order not confusion. God is over the Kingdom of Light, but we see a situation of the Spirit of God hovering over the face of the deep in darkness. Of

---

[9] Elohim is a Hebrew word that denotes "God" or "godhood". It is one of the most common names for God in the Old Testament, appearing over 2,500 times in the Tanakh. — https://www.gotquestions.org/meaning-of-Elohim.html

[2] Tranquility in Eden, Then the Temptation

course, God is almighty and powerful, who transcends everything, but a combination of darkness, formlessness, and emptiness are far from the ways of God.

It's important to point out that angels were created before the beginning of the world. Among the created angels was a high-ranking *cherubim*[10] called Lucifer. Ezekiel expounds:

You were the seal of perfection, full of wisdom and perfect in beauty.

Ezekiel 28:12

Lucifer (meaning "the morning star" and "bearer of knowledge") became corrupted.

---

[10] Cherubim/cherubs are angelic beings involved in the worship and praise of God. The cherubim are first mentioned in the Bible in Genesis 3:24, "After He drove the man out, He placed on the east side of the Garden of Eden cherubim and a flaming sword flashing back and forth to guard the way to the tree of life." Prior to his rebellion, Satan was a cherub (Ezekiel 28:12-15). —
https://www.gotquestions.org/cherubim.html

How?

Isaiah the prophet put it this way:

How you have fallen from heaven, morning star, son of the dawn! You have been cast down to the earth, you who once laid low the nations! You said in your heart, I will ascend to the heavens; I will raise my throne above the stars of God, I will sit enthroned on the mount of assembly, on the utmost heights of Mount Zaphon[11].

Isaiah 14:12-13

Clearly, Lucifer the devil attempted to stage a coup in the Kingdom of Heaven, inviting wrath from

---

[11] Mount Aqraa, also known as Jabal al-Aqraa, Zaphon in the Bible, and Mount Casius to the Greeks, is a limestone mountain located on the Syrian-Turkish border near the mouth of the Orontes River on the Mediterranean Sea. —https://religion.fandom.com/wiki/Mount_Aqraa

[2] Tranquility in Eden, Then the Temptation

God Almighty in the process. He was banished from the sanctuary of Heaven. Because he was a high-ranking angel, he had subordinate angels under him that were complicit in the cardinal sin of wanting to usurp power.

Extreme pride and arrogance predicated on account of his beauty was the precursor to his perverted mind. Ezekiel the prophet corroborates:

> *Your heart became proud on account of beauty, and you corrupted your wisdom because of your splendor. So I threw you to the earth, I made a spectacle of you before kings.*
>
> *Ezekiel 28:17*

Notice that the devil is wise, but corrupt in his wisdom. It's this situation that brought about the chaos in Genesis 1:2. It was never the intention of

God to create the heavens and earth and leave them empty.

Prophet Isaiah delineates:

For this is what the Lord says- He who created the heavens, He is God, He who fashioned and made the earth, He founded it, He did not create it to be empty, but formed it to be inhabited- He says: I am the Lord and there is no other.

Isaiah 45:18

This could be interpreted to mean that between Genesis 1:1 and Genesis 1:2 there were already inhabitants on Earth that were consumed by the events leading up to the banishing of the devil from Heaven, resulting in a formless and empty Earth. In

[2] Tranquility in Eden, Then the Temptation

reference to Genesis 1:2, Charles Spurgeon[12] had this to say:

> *When God began to arrange this world in order, it was shrouded in darkness, and it had been reduced to what we call, for want of a better name, 'chaos.' This is just the condition of every soul of man when God begins to deal with him in His grace; it is formless, and empty of all good things.*

Important to note is that Lucifer fell from Heaven *before* Adam was created and given dominion over Earth.

---

[12] Charles Haddon Spurgeon, also known as the "Prince of Preachers," was a Victorian, Calvinistic, Baptist minister who preached approximately 3600 sermons, wrote dozens of books, oversaw ministries to the poor and orphans, and raised up new pastors. — https://theblazingcenter.com/2018/10/charles-spurgeon-quotes.html

Eventually, the Spirit of God reinstated order by speaking light into existence on day one, translating into night and day. Interestingly, the sun and moon were created on day four to give physical light. So what kind of light came into existence on day one? I believe this light is representative of the glory of God, and bears a supernatural divine essence. The firmament separating the waters above from the waters below was created on day two. On day three, morning and evening, God followed with the separation of waters on the ground, leading to the appearance of land and seas.

Realms or spaces defined the creation of the first three days. Continuing His work of creation, God spoke into existence things to fill up the realms created in the first three days. Still on day three, He called forth vegetation from the ground, consisting of seed-bearing plants and trees that bear fruit with seeds, according to their kinds.

On day four, and the sun and moon were created to govern day and night as well as seasons. On day five God called forth birds and marine creatures, each according to their kind. On day six God spoke into existence creatures that move along the ground, each according to their kind.

[2] Tranquility in Eden, Then the Temptation

Saving the best for last, He molded mankind from the dust of the Earth. He breathed His Spirit into him, and he became a living soul.

So the work of creation was over in six days, and God rested on the seventh day. Notice that all other creatures—birds, fish, and animals—were created according to their kind. *Only man was created in the image of God, not according to his kind*.

How?

"Breath" in Hebrew refers to *Ruach for Spirit*[13], meaning God breathed His Spirit into man, implying Adam was the essence of God. As the image of God, man has spirituality, morality, and personality. This is substantiated by the incarnation of the Second Person in the Trinity, Jesus. And Jesus was able to add humanity to His Deity because mankind is compatible with God.

When you study scripture you will also notice in Genesis 1 that God commanded even the fish and birds to be fruitful and increase in number.

---

[13] Ruach (pronounced roo-akh) is the Hebrew word for spirit, breath, or wind. When spoken, the word engages one's breath and lungs. The first mention of Ruach in the Bible is in the very first chapter of Genesis – Genesis 1:2 —https://firmisrael.org/learn/ruach-the-hebrew-word-for-holy-spirit/

Similarly, He commanded mankind to increase in number and fill the Earth. However, the decree to ruler over other creations is only unique to humankind. I believe this is integral to the identity of mankind.

The Bible says:

Now no shrub had yet appeared on the earth and no plant hat yet sprung up, for the Lord God had not sent rain on the earth and there was no one to work the ground.

Genesis 2:5

Clearly, the dominion and rulership was to incorporate the concept of *work*. To carry out rulership, leadership, management, control, and authority on behalf of God calls for intercourse, companionship, and fellowship of spirit man with the Spirit of God. Therefore, fellowship and work

[2] Tranquility in Eden, Then the Temptation

are central to the identity of man as the image of God.

The Bible says:

Now the Lord God had planted a garden in the east, in Eden, and there put the man he had formed.

Genesis 2:8

Once in the garden, first man Adam was instructed to work the garden—that is, to cultivate and manage it. Adam was free to eat from any tree in the garden, except one.

Moses explained it this way:

> *But you must not eat from the tree of the knowledge of good and evil, for when you eat from it you will certainly die.*
>
> Genesis 2:17

Intuitively, "die" was present in the garden but without a sting.

Thus far, Adam, the male spirit-man, was out and about in the garden by himself. Instructions on work and the command to stay away from the tree in the middle of the garden were received by him alone. Next, we see Adam exercise dominion and stewardship by naming all the species, however, he found none with the same essence. You would expect that with unhindered and direct communication with God coupled with rulership and stewardship, Adam was short of nothing. However, God observed that male-man was lonely.

While in a slumber, the Lord God drew female-man from male-man, Adam. Once awake, Adam

[2] Tranquility in Eden, Then the Temptation

noticed the creature before him. Instantly he opined:

This is flesh of flesh and bone of my bones, and she shall be called woman.

Genesis 2:23

It's vital to understand that both male and female bear the image of God, and together are to carry out the dominion requirement. Now, dominion or rulership is about influence, control, power, and authority premised on the Spirit of God communing with the spirit of male and female, collectively called *man*. Influence of God is the Kingdom of God on Earth. God is spirit and should be worshipped in spirit and truth.

REDISCOVERING IDENTITY

> *God is spirit, and his worshipers must worship in the Spirit and in truth.*
>
> John 4:24

Man the spirit that is unseen required a physical body to operate on Earth, which is physical. Hence, the need for two tangible houses that are male and female to accommodate man the spirit. And whatever God calls for, God provides. Therefore, the clarion call of dominion from God to humanity implies the nature of man has inherent attributes that make dominion possible.

Humans are the only creation with a nature or identity capable of worshipping God. Animals lack the essence for fellowship or communion with God. The stars, moon, and sun fall short of having an essence that fellowships with God. Angels are incapable of dominion because they are not created in the image of God. Additionally, they lack a physical body which is a necessary requirement to exist and operate in the physical universe. That's

[2] Tranquility in Eden, Then the Temptation

why the devil and demons are illegitimate occupants of earth. Only by inhabiting a body (human or animal) can they be effective.

I can state emphatically that God Himself who is faithful to His promise of letting mankind dominate His creation, excuses himself from the dominion mandate. Somewhere in Genesis 1:26, God asserts, "… so that they may rule…"

Clearly, God leaves mankind alone to have dominion.

Awestruck by the pre-eminence of man, David the Psalmist remarks:

REDISCOVERING IDENTITY

> *What is mankind that you are mindful of them, human beings that you care for them? You have made them little lower than angels [some translation say Elohim] and crowned them with glory and honor. You have made them rulers over the works of your hands; you put everything under their feet: all flocks and herds, and the animals of the wild, the birds in the sky, and the fish in the sea, all that swim the paths of the seas.*
>
> *Psalms 8:4-9*

King David seems to wonder that when compared to other majestic creations like the heavens, the stars, and the moon, man seems too small or unworthy of consideration, yet God crowned him with glory and honor. A closer look at creation shows that the essence of animals is just the same as the ground they came from. Similarly,

[2] Tranquility in Eden, Then the Temptation

the essence of marine creatures is the same as the water they live in. In composition, plants too are same as the ground they came from. Close observation shows the stars have the same components as the firmament they were called from by God. And when it came to man, God turned to Himself. Therefore, what is in God is in man.

I am not implying humans are completely identical and equal to God, however of significance, they bear His essence.

For instance, God is love and fulfills this attribute through companionship with man. Parallel to this is the companionship between male and female. Love is a necessity for normal functioning between male and female, as it was between Adam and Eve before *the Fall*[14].

Truthfulness is another attribute that defined mankind prior to the Fall. Knowledge of the truth is necessary to exercise dominion. Where mankind is lacking in love and truth, he or she malfunctions. Dependence and obedience to God was the default

---

[14] The Fall of Man is a term used in Christianity to describe the transition of the first man and woman from a state of innocent obedience to God to a state of guilty disobedience. — https://en.wikipedia.org/wiki/Fall_of_man

set up for Adam and Eve which made it possible to exercise the will of God. Obedience to God's law is paramount for manifestation of the true identity of mankind. Adam and eve were required to be obedient. Paul the apostle summarized the essence of spirit man like this:

But the fruit of the Spirit is love, joy, peace, forbearance, kindness, goodness, faithfulness, gentleness, and self-control. Against such things there is no law.

Galatians 5:22-23

Pre-rebellion, Adam and Eve inherently had these attributes which comprise the true identity of mankind. However, an out-of-position cherubim named Lucifer happened to engage Eve one day:

[2] Tranquility in Eden, Then the Temptation

> *Now the serpent was more crafty than any of the wild animals the LORD God had made. He said to the woman, "Did God really say, 'You must not eat from any tree in the garden'?"*
>
> *Genesis 3:1*

Remember, Adam was given direct instructions to never eat from the *tree of knowledge of good and evil* before Eve ever came into the picture. So I believe the devil clearly approached Eve because he figured the direct recipient of the command may have been hard to persuade. However, Eve responded to the devil that the tree in the middle of the garden was off limits. The devil knew the consequence if man should eat from the tree in the middle of the garden, so he persisted:

REDISCOVERING IDENTITY

For God knows that when you eat from it your eyes will be opened, and you will be like God, knowing good and evil.

Genesis 3:5

Man ate of the tree and activated *death* in the process. Earlier I pointed out that "die" was present but without sting, however with mankind's disobedience "die" got its sting. In the process mankind fell from rulership of his domain. Man's greatest sin was *diffidence*—being too timid or shy to recognize his power granted by God, call it an identity problem. He was already like God because in the image of God both male and female were created.

[3]

Humankind's Enduring Image & Likeness of God Beyond the Fall

In the fall of man lies the seed of his redemption, for only in darkness can light shine brightest.

— Unknown

FROM THE PREVIOUS chapter, we observe that man chose to activate his will, call it the power of choice, by disobeying God. It's with the human will that we choose to serve God or not. Immediately,

REDISCOVERING IDENTITY

man was exiled from paradise to the wilderness. Immediately, man transitioned from the Garden of Eden to Earth as we know it. Gone were the vegetation and trees that were pleasant to the eye and good for food. Now, mankind had to deal with a world of uncertainty. Paradise was defined by pleasure, abundance—call it eternal provision, but now scarcity, uncertainty, sweat, blood, disease, tears, and death defined humankind's world.

> *Cursed is the ground because of you, through painful toil you will eat food from it all the days of your life. It will produce thorns and thistles for you, and you will eat the plants of the field.*
>
> Genesis 3:17-18

Clearly, this predicted more difficulty for man as labor and effort would be required to pluck out weeds or unwanted plants. Earlier I expounded on

[3] Humankind's Enduring Image & Likeness of God Beyond the Fall

dominion as representative of man's authority and identity as the image of God, which leads to the question, "Is humankind's identity as the image of God still intact after the Fall?"

After expulsion from the Garden of Eden, mankind's innocence was replaced by a sense of shame and guilt. Furthermore, humankind's true wisdom that was premised on the Spirit of God dwelling within mankind was replaced by a wisdom purely dependent on man's conscience. Man's status as the perfect image of God was reduced to a degraded or compromised image. Still, man bore the image of God. This is corroborated by this account:

REDISCOVERING IDENTITY

This is the written account of Adam's family line. When God created mankind, he made them in the likeness of God... When Adam had lived 130 years, he had a son in his own likeness, in his own image, and he named him Seth.

Genesis 5:1-3

We see that Adam had Seth after the Fall, but Seth was in the likeness of Adam. Important to note here is that Adam was in the likeness of God, and so was Adam's son. Somewhere it is written that Adam went on to live 930 years, implying that after begetting Seth, Adam lived another 800 years. You may be wondering if he should have died after eating of the tree of knowledge of good and evil.

[3] Humankind's Enduring Image & Likeness of God Beyond the Fall

> *Altogether, Adam lived a total of 930 years, and then he died.*
>
> *Genesis 5:5*

God promised that humankind would surely die if he ate of the tree of knowledge of good and evil, however, hundreds of years later Adam was still alive. This can mean only one thing: God's implication of "die" was not a physical death. Remember that prior to sin and declaring independence, mankind epitomized the perfect *imago Dei*, Latin for image of God. However, the Spirit of God deserted mankind after sinning, meaning that man is dead without the Spirit of God living in him.

This is why every human is born into bondage or a world of darkness, a condition that can only be overcome through being born again in spirit. (More on this in the upcoming chapters.) And for man to manifest his true *imago Dei*, the Spirit of God has to superintend over the other faculties of man, that is, body, soul, and spirit. Void of the Holy Spirit, man is a lesser image of God.

Why a lesser image? Obviously, mankind can't now manifest the true image of God and likeness, and dominion is now shrouded in a blanket of uncertainty. However, humankind still is a *one-in-three*, just like the Holy Trinity. The Holy Trinity is one-in-three distinct personalities of God the Father, the Son, and the Holy Spirit. Equal but distinct. This Trinity thrives in unity. Now, humankind is the only other one-in-three being.

The spirit is the highest expression of mankind, and it's in the spirit that man is able to fellowship and worship God. So the spirit places man in the "god" class. David the Psalmist put it this way:

I said, you are "gods", you are all sons of the Most High.

Psalm 82:6

---

[3] Humankind's Enduring Image & Likeness of God Beyond the Fall

Animals have no spirit at all. Neither do plants as well as other inanimate creatures. Now, *the soul of man* is the spiritual component of man, aligned with his body. It's in the soul that man has capacity for advanced thought processing and emotions. And the *human will* is part and parcel of the soul.

Man's soul is eternal in the sense that it lives on when man dies. Animals have a soul too, however their soul is entirely intertwined with their nature. Meaning that when animals die, their soul dies with them. Also, the souls of animals are not capable of rationality. I can also state that angels don't have a soul, but have a spirit as they lack a physical body.

Living souls can only exist in physical bodies. Plants and other inanimate creatures have no souls. Man, like animals, has a body. It's with the body that man can smell, see, touch, feel, taste, and hear. Higher animals are capable of this, too. Without the Spirit of God, without self-control, mankind would function at the level of animals. Why? Because he is driven by the desires of the flesh, no more than an animal.

REDISCOVERING IDENTITY

Still, corrupted man bears the image of God. Even after the Noahic floods, it's evident man is still the *imago Dei*.

The Bible says:

Whoever sheds human blood, by humans shall their blood be shed; for in the image of God has God made mankind.

Genesis 9:6

Clearly, the only fitting punishment for killing another human is death, so says God. This is because man is created in the nature of God. Therefore, murdering another human is a direct assault on God himself. It can be deduced that the Fall didn't wipe out the essence of God in man, instead it limited man from fully expressing the imago Dei. And in his limited capacity, we see man is still capable of rationality and freedom of will.

[3] Humankind's Enduring Image & Likeness of God Beyond the Fall

And in his fallen capacity, mankind still harbors knowledge of his own existence, call it the knowledge of oneself as a conscious being. It's these hallmarks that speak to the personhood of man which was extant in man even after the Fall. For mankind to carry out the royal function of Kingdom of God rulership (dominion) on Earth, the Holy Spirit has to govern over the personhood of man, resulting in the full manifestation of the imago Dei, dominion, so to speak.

When the governor, that is, the spirit of God is absent from mankind, a limited or lesser version of the imago Dei is manifested. In the primeval[15] era we see mankind engaging in hunting, fishing, and agriculture, which is an expression of dominion. In the modern era, man continues to demonstrate dominion in the areas of science, technology, healthcare, transport, and so on. Nonetheless, fallen man is a sinful man.

You can say a man is untamed without the Spirit of God. Untamed man suffers from a lack of self-control. Untamed man harbors resentment,

---

[15] Of or belonging to the first ages; original; primal; primitive. — https://www.wordnik.com/words/primeval

jealousy, and hatred, instead of love. In his fallen nature, man lacks consistency in the areas of kindness, goodness, honesty, love, patience, and gentleness. What we see is the inconsistency prevalent in the attitude or essence of man.

James put it this way:

> *With the tongue, we praise our Lord and Father, and with it, we curse human beings, who have been made in God's likeness.*
>
> *James 3:9*

Sinful man leans towards doing evil. Sinful man is short of righteousness. In his fallen nature man struggles to being holy. This underscores the fact that man lost innocence, righteousness, holiness, and obedience to God. This is corroborated by Moses the lawgiver:

[3] Humankind's Enduring Image & Likeness of God Beyond the Fall

> *Now Cain said to his brother Abel, let's go out to the field. While they were in the field, Cain attacked his brother Abel and killed him.*
>
> *Genesis 4:8*

No longer the bearer of God's authentic image, we can see in his compromised imago Dei, Cain exhibits deception, evil, unholiness, a lack of righteousness. A degraded image of God, so to speak. Compromised integrity and dignity are also at full display, as he commits the first act of murder by man in scripture. This epitomizes the spirit of rebellion inherent in fallen man, independent from God, yet he was created to be totally obedient and dependent on God, so as to fully manifest the imago Dei.

One day, I was at work and decided to stroll in the parking lot on my lunch break. A few minutes into my break, I received a call from my co-worker that one of the company associates had passed out in the parking lot. I quickly rushed to the scene to help out. No sooner had I reached the scene than three other employees joined in to help.

This employee was on the ground and unable to respond to speech, so I checked for a pulse. Fortunately, the pulse was present. Immediately, an emergency call was placed, and an ambulance showed up in under 15 minutes, which quickly took him to the local emergency room.

The sad part is that this employee chose to drink 375 ml of Jack Daniel's whiskey during his break, while still at work. In my mind, I wondered, *How is an individual dominated by the very thing he was commanded by God to have dominion over?* Self-control is one of the gifts of the Spirit of God but is absent in sinful man. Alcohol is a derivative of fermented fruits. (Part of what was given to Adam to dominate were fruit- and seed-bearing plants). Void of the Spirit of God's guidance, man is incapable of genuine dominion and man's identity as a creature in the image of God is compromised.

Now, if mankind still retained the image of God after the Fall, the question may arise, What did he lose? From Genesis 1:26, we can deduce that

[3] Humankind's Enduring Image & Likeness of God Beyond the Fall

"image and likeness" were closely tied to "dominion." Therefore, man fell from rulership, and from dominion, which is the Kingdom of God's influence on Earth.

Still, we see Cain demonstrating some rulership after the Fall.

How?

The Bible says:

Cain made love to his wife, and she became pregnant and gave birth to Enoch. Cain was then building a city, and he named it after his son Enoch.

Genesis 4:17

Not only did he build a city and name it after his son, but it's the first city ever built by man in scripture. A demonstration of rulership, but this rulership was not under the guidance of the Holy Spirit. True and authentic rulership is premised on a relationship that is in alignment with God.

Obviously, Cain had a history of defiance against God. Later, we also see Cain's great-great-grandson Lamech marry two wives, in addition to murdering a man.

> *Lamech said to his wives, "Adah and Zillah, listen to me; wives of Lamech, hear my words. I have killed a man for wounding me, a young man for injuring me."*
>
> Genesis 4:23

Clearly, when a man is in a relationship that is out of position with God, then his relationships with others are also out of position. Therefore, after sinning and rebelling against God, humankind's relationship with God was out of position. Also, humankind's relationship with other

[3] Humankind's Enduring Image & Likeness of God Beyond the Fall

people is out of position or compromised. Additionally, mankind's relationship with the non-human creation that is supposed to be under his feet is out of order and compromised. When we compromise, we accept standards that are lower.

This is corroborated by the following account:

The man said, the woman you put here with me, she gave me some fruit from the tree, and I ate it.

Genesis 3:12

Clearly, we see Adam's relationship out of position with God and he quickly proceeds to shift blame to the woman, a disharmony between the two, so to speak. When man's relationship with God is in disharmony, other relationships too are out of order. Previously, I mentioned the consequence of the rebellion which resulted in a cursed ground characterized by thorns and thistles.

This shows man's relationship is not in harmony with what he's supposed to govern. Hence, mankind's identity as the imago Dei is corrupted.

The Apostle Paul corroborates this:

> *But there's a place where someone has testified: what is mankind that you are mindful of them, a son of man that you care for them? You made them a little lower than angels; you crowned them with glory and honor and put everything under their feet. In putting everything under them, God left nothing that is not subject to them. Yet at present, we do not see everything subject to them.*
>
> *Hebrews 2:6-8*

[4]

Shadows of Humankind's Redemption

God's redemption is a symphony of grace, where broken chords of humanity find restoration, and harmonize with the melody of divine love.

— *Unknown*

A CLOSER LOOK at creation reveals that everything God created has potential, and everything with potential has purpose. For instance, in Genesis 1 we see that all vegetation called forth by the creator consisted of seed-bearing plants, and fruit-bearing trees. Now, each seed has potential to bring forth a tree, or simply put, in each seed is a tree.

Or is it?

Potentially, every seed brings forth a tree with fruit that contains a seed or seeds, which in turn have the potential to bring forth trees, and trees constitute a forest. Stated another way, *in every seed is a forest*. Parallel to this is the seed that was in the loins of Adam. In Adam was all humanity, and when God was speaking to Adam, He was speaking to the seed in the loins of Adam, which seed had the potential to bring forth millions if not billions of people. As we speak, there are 8 billion people on the face of Earth, *all from the seed of Adam*. So when Adam sinned, all mankind sinned. That's why we are all born into sin, and we require redemption or restoration into our originality.

Immediately after the Fall, God embarked on a redemption program to restore mankind back to Kingdom rulership tied to the *imago Dei*. This redemption was also to restore man back into his God-ordained purpose. Furthermore, redemption

[4] Shadows of Humankind's Redemption

was to reconcile man back into original leadership. Original leadership is about harnessing one's God-given gifts, talents, or abilities. In doing so, one manifests his or her true identity. God stated categorically that there would be animosity between the woman's seed and the serpent.

And I will put enmity
between you and the woman,
and between your offspring
and hers;
he will crush your head,
and you will strike his heel.

Genesis 3:15

Anatomically and physiologically, a woman can't produce a seed as it is a man's duty provide seed in propagation. Therefore, God was referring to the virgin birth of the Savior through Mary that was to come 4,000 years after the Fall of Man.

God loves mankind so much that even after their rebellion, He works on the reconciliation of man. And let me point this out—Lucifer and his cadres had fallen before the rebellion of man against God. However, nowhere in the scripture did God ever provide a redemptive program for fallen angels. Why? Only man bears the image of God, not even angels. God loves Himself so much that he had to redeem His image.

Also important to note is that the Fall of Man didn't take God by surprise. Why? The Bible says:

He was chosen before the creation of the world, but was revealed in these last times for your sake.

1 Peter 1:20

For further exegesis on this, we see in Revelation:

[4] Shadows of Humankind's Redemption

All inhabitants of the earth will worship the beast—all whose names have not been written in the Lamb's book of life, the lamb who was slain from the creation of the world.

Revelation 13:8

Clearly, God foresaw the Fall of Man, after all He is the Omniscient One.

For God so loved the world that he gave his one and only Son, that whoever believes in him shall not perish but have eternal life.

John 3:16

In the aftermath of mankind's rebellion, God made clothing from animals skins for Adam and Eve.

The Lord God made garments of skin for Adam and his wife and clothed them.

Genesis 3:21

Before expulsion from the Garden, God had to clothe mankind in garments of animal skin. Deep analysis of this implies that animals were sacrificed by God to dress naked man. There was a need for the shedding of blood to cleanse mankind. I can picture blood-dripping animal skin over them, which served as a partial cleansing or partial redemption. The blood of sinful man was impure in that another person's blood couldn't be used even as a partial cleanser. So much so that animal blood was necessary for this temporal act of redemption.

[4] Shadows of Humankind's Redemption

Remember that Adam and Eve tried to cover themselves with fig leaves, but leaves lack blood. In similar fashion our great works are not sufficient to redeem us. An animal had to die so as to provide suspension of sin. Shedding of blood was paramount for partial suspension of sin. The great Apostle asserts:

In fact, the law requires that nearly everything be cleansed with blood, and without the shedding of blood there is no forgiveness.

Hebrews 9:22

I believe Adam understood the need for animal sacrifice in a bid to be in right standing with God. Later we see Abel offering a lamb as sacrifice to God, while Cain offers a plant-based sacrifice. No wonder God was pleased with Abel's sacrifice, because it entailed the shedding of animal blood.

On the other hand, Cain's sacrifice was rejected, Why? Because plants have no blood in them.

Blood symbolizes life as well as death. To put this in perspective, anatomically and physiologically, a human body requires blood to deliver oxygen and nutrients for sustenance. On the other hand, sickness comes to the body through blood. Once disease-causing agents enter a body they are transported by blood throughout the entire body. And a body overwhelmed by disease dies. However, introduction of disease-free or clean blood into a diseased body can reverse the course of the illness.

For instance, if one suffers from leukemia then a blood transfusion from a healthy individual is required for remission. Notice that blood from another leukemia patient is of no benefit. This is why the pure and spotless blood of Jesus Christ had to be shed for our sake.

To God be the glory, power, and dominion.

The Bible says:

[4] Shadows of Humankind's Redemption

For to us a child is born, to us a Son is given, and the government will be on His shoulders. And He will be called Wonderful Counsellor, Mighty God, Everlasting Father, Prince of Peace.

Isaiah 9:6

A clear shadow of what was to come, so to speak. To Mary a child (Jesus) was to be born, however, the Son (Christ) was to be given by God the Father. Important to note is that "the government" was to be on His shoulders. In lucid terms, the government is the Kingdom of God. It's exactly what Adam lost and was to be restored by Jesus Christ. Adam fell from Kingdom rulership, not from Heaven.

The whole redemption program in scripture is geared toward restoration of man back into dominion premised on the influence of God. This is necessary because man is the purpose and end of creation. The identity of man is predicated on his ability to exercise dominion over the nonhuman creation. True and genuine dominion is only possible with the guidance of the Spirit of God.

Throughout the Old Testament, several scriptures foreshadow the coming of the Messiah, whose primary purpose was to redeem mankind. Now, "testament" refers to "testimony," which is a legal term. Normally, in courts of law a witness provides testimony to establish a truthful account. Testimony eliminates a neutral position and establishes commitment. Scripture is founded on testimony inspired by the Spirit of God. The Word of God is the truth.

Here are some of the Old Testament scriptures that in a way are a shadow of the reality (redemption) that was to come:

[4] Shadows of Humankind's Redemption

Therefore the Lord Himself will give you a sign: behold, a virgin will be with a child and bear a son, and she will call His name Immanuel.

Isaiah 7:14

No longer will they teach their neighbor, or say to one another, know the Lord, because they will all know me from the least of them to the greatest, declares the Lord. For I will forgive their wickedness and will remember their sins no more.

Jeremiah 31:34

REDISCOVERING IDENTITY

Rejoice greatly, Daughter Zion! Shout, Daughter Jerusalem! See your King comes to you righteous and victorious lowly and riding on a donkey.

Zechariah 9:9

But you, Bethlehem Ephrathah, though you are small among the clans of Judah, out of you will come for me one who will be ruler over Israel whose origins are from old, from ancient times.

Micah 5:2

From the above scriptures it is known that the Savior will be born of a virgin. It is also known that His arrival into Jerusalem will be on a donkey, blameless, and having salvation. And we are told

[4] Shadows of Humankind's Redemption

that He will be born in Bethlehem. Truth be told, there are many more scriptures in the Old Testament pointing towards redemption of mankind, and outlining them will be a book of its own.

As a matter of fact, the whole Old Testament constitutes the salvation program of man. Mathew the Apostle corroborates this:

> *Do not think that I have come to abolish the Law or the Prophets; I have not come to abolish them but to fulfill them. For truly I tell you, until heaven and earth disappear, not the smallest letter, not the least stroke of a pen, will by any means disappear from the Law until everything is accomplished.*
>
> *Mathew 5:17-18*

"The Law" herein refers to the first five books of the Bible, and "the Prophets" refers to books starting from Joshua to Malachi. Jesus Christ unequivocally asserted that Old Testament scripture points to Him and He fulfills it.

One of the shadows of redemption in the Old Testament is the story of Abraham. Abraham so believed in God that he was credited as being righteous. Abraham and his wife Sarah were without child. Actually, they were past childbearing age when God promised Abraham he would have a child. Sarah, Abraham's wife, dismissed this promise with laughter, and who would blame her? She was barren and old.

Fast forward, Abraham and Sarah welcomed their son, Isaac. Sarah was 90 years old, and Abraham was 100 years old. God had declared that Abraham would be made into a great nation. However, God commanded Abraham to offer Isaac as a sacrifice. Trusting God, Abraham proceeded with 12-year-old Isaac to the top of the mountain so as to fulfill God's command. Before Abraham could carry out the act of sacrificing Isaac, God provided a lamb that was in the nearby thicket. This lamb foreshadowed what was to come—that is,

[4] Shadows of Humankind's Redemption

Jesus Christ, as the Lamb of God who takes away the sin of the world.

Salvation of mankind was paramount to God. Why? I am afraid to say this, but I will go ahead and say it anyway: God's program to redeem man is not because He felt sorry for man, it is because God loves Himself so much. I am not saying God has no feelings of pity on man, certainly not, because God is mercy. However, God loves Himself such that He couldn't stomach a defaced or compromised image of His.

Earlier on, I expounded that God is love, and for love to be fulfilled calls for a relationship with one of a kind. This is the primary reason God decided to create mankind in His own image—for fellowship, so to speak. Out of love for Himself, He embarked on a mission to salvage mankind in order to restore His image. If you remember, God decreed that on the day mankind ate of the tree of knowledge of good and evil, he would surely die. In other words, the choice was set between life or death, premised on a condition of obedience to God.

Consequently, man activated death through disobedience. Now, man had to pay the price, or did he?

For God so loved the world, that he gave his only begotten Son, that whosoever believeth in Him should not perish, but have everlasting life.

John 3:16

It's probable that this is the best-known scripture, and for good reason. I don't know of anyone who chose to die in place of another who committed a wrong. I don't care how much someone loves you, they can never switch places to pay the price for your wrongdoing. But we see Jesus Christ shoulder the blame of mankind, and pay the price in full.

Apostle Paul testified:

[4] Shadows of Humankind's Redemption

But we do see Jesus who was made lower than the angels for a little while, now crowned with glory and honor because he suffered death, so that by the grace of God He might taste death for everyone.

Hebrews 2:9

REDISCOVERING IDENTITY

[5]

In Redemption, the Past is Forgiven, and the Future is Salvaged

---

*The weak can never forgive.
Forgiveness is the attribute
of the strong.*

— *Mahatma Gandhi*

FORGIVENESS IS A pool that a child can swim in with ease, but tough for an adult to wade. Conflict is part and parcel of human relationships. Almost every family has estranged relatives. It's easy for humankind to harbor resentment and anger against one another than to simply say, "I forgive you." I know of people who hold on to a grudge for donkey years. Makes me wonder if there are any benefits to this spirit of unforgiveness. Certainly not, and God forbid.

As a Healthcare professional, I learned that physiologically almost all the major organs of the human body have a way to eliminate toxic substances. For instance, the kidney via its filtration system eliminates waste from the body. Among its many functions the liver eliminates harmful substances via bile and blood that are eliminated from the body via digestive tract and kidney. The integument[16] through its pores eliminates waste via sweat. Clearly, the physical body was designed by the Creator with mechanisms in place to eliminate waste from the body.

Nonetheless, the spirit and soul of man lack a mechanism to automatically let go of a toxic

---

[16] integument, noun. in·teg·u·ment in-'te-gyə-mənt: something that covers or encloses especially an enveloping layer (such as a skin, membrane, or cuticle) of an organism or one of its parts — https://www.merriam-webster.com/dictionary/integument

[5] In Redemption, the Past is Forgiven, and the Future is Salvaged

attitude, creating a possibility of toxic buildup in the heart.

Jesus once said to his disciples:

Don't you see that whatever enters the mouth goes into the stomach and then out of the body? But the things that come out of a person's mouth come from the heart, and these defile them.

Mathew 15:17-18

Here Jesus stresses the fact that the body eliminates what goes into it, but the heart, defined by a toxic environment, defiles a person. The heart refers to the soul, which is the seat of the subconscious mind. I am reminded of a remarkable story of forgiveness. There are moments that happen to us, good or bad, that are frozen in time.

For Dr. Robert Smith, it is about what transpired on October 30, 2010 at 11:56 pm.

On that day four young men stormed their way into a restaurant where Dr. Robert Smith's son was working. In this attempted robbery, one of the four pulled the trigger and shot Dr. Smith's son. The promising life of this young man came to an end at only 34 years old. Meanwhile, the 17-year-old who committed the murder ended up in prison. Inspired by Spirit of God, Dr. Smith decided to write to the young man in prison who took his son's life. Two years passed without a response, and then one day a reply from prison manifested.

It was one full of remorse and regret. The young man in prison thanked Dr. Smith for forgiving him. Dr. Smith was moved to make the remarkable gesture of forgiving the murderer of his son, on the insightful grounds that moving past this sad experience required *forgiveness*. In forgiving, Dr. Smith chose to love instead of hate. He chose to make peace instead of disharmony. Dr. Smith demonstrated the essence of being in the image of God. God is love, and as the *imago Dei* mankind has the capacity to love.

[5] In Redemption, the Past is Forgiven, and the Future is Salvaged

When we don't love, we malfunction and don't reflect our true identity, the *imago Dei*.

The Bible says:

For if you forgive other people when they sin against you, your heavenly Father will also forgive you. But if you do not forgive others their sins, your Father will not forgive your sins.

Mathew 6:14-15

Forgiveness promotes reconciliation. Forgiveness promotes restoration. And redemption is impossible without forgiveness. Only via forgiveness did mankind get a second chance and was salvaged by the author and perfector of our faith, Jesus Christ. The lamb of God, free from sin, chose to take on the sin of mankind so as to restore man back into Kingdom rulership.

REDISCOVERING IDENTITY

Peter the Apostle asserts:

He himself bore our sins in His body on the cross, so that we might die to sins and live for righteousness; by His wounds you have been healed.

1 Peter 2:24

God forgave our sins by sacrificing His one and only begotten son. This shows how special mankind is to God.

[5] In Redemption, the Past is Forgiven, and the Future is Salvaged

But God demonstrates His own love for us in this: while we were still sinners, Christ died for us.

Romans 5:8

Because we sinned, it was fitting that we pay the price. We deserved to die, but God took our place and paid the price in full. God's love for mankind is inexhaustible. Put another way, God's love, mercy, and grace supersedes our sins. Because of our "mess" God the Father sent us the "Mess-iah." In forgiveness, man is redeemed and reconciled back to what he was created to be. Man is restored back into an authentic *imago Dei*. All we are required to do is to believe, and by the grace of God we become born again in the Spirit.

Once you accept Jesus Christ as your Savior, daily you are swimming in an endless ocean of God's Love, mercy, and grace. You are redeemed and restored as a child of God. As believers we are offspring of Our Father in Heaven. And we get to share in the Kingdom rulership on behalf of God.

Remember that Kingdom rulership or dominion constitutes harnessing the talents, gifts, and abilities that are inherent within you. Dominion is second to fellowship as the primary reasons for the creation of man. So, when we effectively fellowship with God and others, coupled with excelling in our areas of gifting, our authority and identity is manifested, implying we are not out of position or alignment in life. We are in order because we are able to realize and fully maximize our potential. Also we operate with an others-centered awareness. And more importantly, we do the will of God that glorifies Him. Faith in God and His grace is all we need. It's not about our own works, lest we boast.

The Apostle Paul gives credence to this matter:

[5] In Redemption, the Past is Forgiven, and the Future is Salvaged

Know that a person is not justified by the works of the law, but by faith in Jesus Christ. So we, too, have put our faith in Christ Jesus that we may be justified by faith in Christ and not by the works of the law, because by the works of the law no one will be justified.

Galatians 2:16

In addition, Paul articulates that:

REDISCOVERING IDENTITY

For it is by grace you have been saved, through faith—and this is not from yourselves, it is the gift of God—not by works, so that no one can boast.

Ephesians 2: 8-9

And in Romans 3: 21-28, Paul drives the point home:

[5] In Redemption, the Past is Forgiven, and the Future is Salvaged

But now apart from the law the righteousness of God has been made known, to which the Law and the Prophets testify. This righteousness is given through faith in Jesus Christ to all who believe. There is no difference between Jew and Gentile, for all have sinned and fall short of the glory of God, and all are justified freely by his grace through the redemption that came by Christ Jesus. God presented Christ as a sacrifice of atonement, through the shedding of his blood—to be received by faith. He did this to demonstrate his righteousness, because in his forbearance he had left the sins committed beforehand unpunished—he did it to demonstrate his righteousness at the present time, so as to be just and the one who justifies those who have faith in Jesus. Where,

> *then, is boasting? It is excluded. Because of what law? The law that requires works? No, because of the law that requires faith. For we maintain that a person is justified by faith apart from the works of the law.*
>
> *Romans 3: 21-28*

God is so good and makes righteousness accessible to all. How? Just by faith and grace, nothing more or less. You don't need a PhD in theology, you don't have to keep up with countless religious rituals and practices, nor climb to the top of Mt. Everest. God's supply of grace and mercy supersedes any demand for sin.

In forgiveness our past is dead, and our future is salvaged. We become new creatures in Christ Jesus. You and I are justified once, and we have to believe without a doubt. The shame is gone, even though we still harbor a feeling of guilt. Actually, guilt is necessary as a moral compass. For without guilt, how can a person differentiate good from

[5] In Redemption, the Past is Forgiven, and the Future is Salvaged

bad? Gradually, we grow in spirit with each passing test or trial. Trials are God's training program to strengthen our faith. Faith is one of the important keys that is necessary for dominion to manifest. And for faith to be effective, it should germinate in the soils of love and truth.

Of great importance is the understanding that God the Father and through Jesus Christ has redeemed us unto to Himself. Why? For Kingdom of Heaven rulership on Earth, so that we can reign on Earth. In doing this we bring Kingdom of Heaven culture on Earth, implying the invisible values, norms, and values of the Kingdom of Heaven manifest on Earth through the visible man.

This is only possible with the Spirit of God communing with the spirit of man, influencing the soul of man in the process which in turn influences the human body, resulting in the manifestation of the true identity of man, the *imago Dei*. The essence is for us to know who we are, and then live out life as children of God. John the Apostle corroborates:

REDISCOVERING IDENTITY

And has made us to be a kingdom and priests to serve His God and Father- to Him be glory and power for ever and ever! Amen.

Revelation 1:6

We are called to be like Jesus Christ who is the perfect model of what it means to be in the image of God. During his ministry on Earth, Jesus Christ demonstrated a priestly and kingly way of life. As Priest, Jesus Christ taught and preached the Kingdom of God message. He always isolated Himself from everyone else and delved into deep prayer to God the Father. As King, Jesus Christ subdued every situation and circumstance as evidenced by His miracles. Whether it was healing the sick, casting out demons, raising the dead, silencing the storm, walking on water, ad infinitum, He did it all.

Did I mention triumphing over death as evidenced by His resurrection? In similar fashion, our calling is to be kings and priests on Earth, now.

[5] In Redemption, the Past is Forgiven, and the Future is Salvaged

You heard me! Jesus promised us to do greater things than He did:

Very truly I tell you, whoever believes in me will do the works I have been doing, and they will do even greater things than these, because I am going to the Father.

John 14:12

It can't be any more lucid and crystal clear than this. Our authentic human identity is about exercising rulership on Earth under the guidelines of the Spirit of God. We are destined to wear two hearts harmoniously, that is, priests and kings, so to speak. In our priestly nature, we engage in seeking the knowledge of God, worshipping and praising God. Studying the Word as well as teaching the Word is part and parcel of our priestly role. At the same time we are to take charge of life being proactive, prioritizing, preparing, and planning. This way we become kings over the circumstances of life. To be effective as kings, we have to wisely use our time. Additionally, we have to prepare and plan for change. And Jesus Christ promised to give us the keys to dominion.

Here are some scriptures concerning our dominion identity:

I will give you the keys of the kingdom of heaven; whatever you bind on earth will be bound in heaven, and whatever you loose on earth will be loosed in heaven.

Mathew 16:19

---

[5] In Redemption, the Past is Forgiven, and the Future is Salvaged

I have given you authority to trample on snakes and scorpions and to overcome all the power of the enemy, nothing will harm you.

Luke 10:19

For the sin of this one man, Adam caused death to rule over many. But even greater is God's wonderful grace and His gift of righteousness, for all who receive it will live in triumph over sin and death through this one man, Jesus Christ.

Romans 5:17

REDISCOVERING IDENTITY

You have made them to be a kingdom and priests to serve our God, and they will reign on the earth.

Revelation 5:10

Now, this presents us a choice between the first Adam and the Last Adam. In the first Adam, we are forever trapped in bondage and resigned to death in the body and spirit. On the other hand, we become born again in Spirit in the Last Adam, new creatures in Christ Jesus destined for eternal life physically and spiritually. The choice is between two men, Adam or Jesus Christ, not between two trees.

My question to you is, "Who will define your identity?" It's my only hope and prayer that you choose the latter.

[6]

Beloved of Christ, the Devil is a Liar

It is not the opinion of others that defines who you are, but your own perception of yourself. Embrace your unique qualities, strengths, and dreams, for it is in your authentic self that you will discover your true identity, and unlock your greatest potential.

— Unknown

REDISCOVERING IDENTITY

SINCE THE DAWN of time, and throughout the ages the physical Earth is the stage where two worlds are caught up in a battle for the soul of man. There's the world of light against one of darkness. Not only that, but the battle is also between good and evil. The spirit and soul of man is forever in a battle of truth against deception.

Paul the Apostle postulates:

> *For our struggle is not against flesh and blood, but against the rulers, against the authorities, against the powers of this dark world and against the spiritual forces of evil in the heavenly realms.*
>
> *Ephesians 6:12*

Our calling is to embrace the salvation offered by Jesus Christ, however, the father of lies—the devil—is unrelenting in his mission to distort, plunder, and destroy mankind. Jesus Christ paid the

[6] Beloved of Christ, the Devil is a Liar

full price to reconcile us back to Himself so that we can experience the transformative power that overcomes the tests and challenges of life. Meanwhile, the tempter-in-chief, the devil, is dedicated to perverting our minds.

In corrupting our souls the devil desires for us to be filled with fear, doubt, hopelessness, and worthlessness. The devil is out to test our flesh—appetites, desires, and cravings. Irrespective of this, we are to remain steadfast in the love and truth of Jesus Christ. In Christ our past is forgiven and no longer should we feel worthless and doubtful. Shame is relegated to the past. In highlighting your failures or areas of weakness the devil capitalizes on ignorance as his main weapon of choice.

How?

For instance, believing in other people's opinions about you is one way the devil attacks you. More often than not, the opinions are from our family members, friends, teachers, coaches, or mentors. These, the very people who are supposed to be a source of encouragement, are often instead a conduit for the tempter's agenda. The result of which is a feeling of insignificance coupled with self-doubt.

An article published in *Tit-Bits Magazine*[17] on September 18, 1897, attests how ignorance is a potent weapon for the devil. It is accredited to one Conan Doyle. Now, Doyle had a friend who set out to test the assumption that in every household is a skeleton in the closet, irrespective of how decent that household may be. His chosen subject for the experiment was none other than a revered Archdeacon of the church. The Archdeacon's reputation was spotless.

So, a telegram was dispatched to the highly respected gentleman from a nearby post office: "All is discovered! Fly at once!" Leading to the disappearance of the Archdeacon, never to be seen again. The moral of this story is that if the Archdeacon's identity was rooted in Jesus Christ, then he would not flee. Why? In Christ we are accepted as we are, a chosen people, so to speak.

---

[17] Tit-Bits from all the interesting Books and Newspapers of the World, more commonly known as Tit-Bits, was a British weekly magazine founded by George Newnes, a founding figure in popular journalism, on 22 October 1881. —https://en.wikipedia.org/wiki/Tit-Bits

[6] Beloved of Christ, the Devil is a Liar

Not only are we chosen, but we were chosen before the foundation of the world.

The devil desires to imprison mankind in a cell of shame. In Christ our past is forgiven and we become new creatures.

The Bible says:

> *For he chose us in Him before the creation of the world to be holy and blameless in His sight. In love He predestined us for adoption to sonship through Jesus Christ, in accordance with his pleasure and will.*
>
> *Ephesians 1: 4-5*

I don't know about you, but this right here authenticates how pre-eminent we are compared to all creation. What this means is that, before God created anything, He chose you. You are second to none compared to all creation. When you understand this, the devil is in trouble. Because the truth you know shall set you free. Before the greater lights were created, you were predestined as children of God. Understanding that you are chosen before any animal, vegetation, or waterbody was ever created underscores that you should be free from any self-doubt regarding who you are. Created before the foundation of the world implies that you are the reason the world was created. And not vice versa.

Meanwhile, the devil is counting on your disbelief to take root. Unyielding is the devil as he gallivants back and forth over Earth looking for who to devour. The devil wants you to believe that you are a reject. Satan pre-occupies you with your past mistakes, torments, and sufferings, hoping that you believe that and see yourself as unworthy and unwelcome. When this happens, you find people doing everything they can to feel accepted by others.

A common scenario is for one to sacrifice their individuality for the sake of fitting into a group. I have observed people doing everything they can to seek validation from others. In this day and age,

[6] Beloved of Christ, the Devil is a Liar

multitudes of people devote their effort, time, and money trying to be like other people. For instance, people identify themselves with what brand of clothing, shoes, or cologne they wear. They feel important wearing someone else's name. Or the kind of car one drives speaks to the essence of who they are. *This is sickness of mind.* Satan is winning because multitudes are highly intoxicated on the ignorance of who they are. The truth is that you are predestined for adoption in God's family.

And Jesus Christ says:

> *... Come, you who are blessed by my Father; take your inheritance, the kingdom prepared for you since the creation of the world.*
>
> Mathew 25:34

This is so amazing—a kingdom inheritance already awaits us because we are children of the Most High. For an inheritance to be accessed, obedience while one waits is required. Additionally, death has to occur for the inheritance to be accessed. Jesus was crucified on the cross for you and me, so that we can access the Kingdom inheritance.

This inheritance refers to the Spirit of God that dwells in those who believe in Jesus Christ. This underscores the love that God the Father and Jesus Christ our Lord have for us. It's the agape[18] kind of love, unconditional and everlasting. On the other hand, the devil works tirelessly to make us feel unloved. He will highlight our struggles so as to overwhelm us or get us feeling depressed. But the devil is a liar, and shouldn't be believed. No matter what suffering you may go through, you were predestined and set apart. Your life is not an experiment, as your days are ordained in the book before any of them ever came to be.

---

[18] agape, /əˈgeɪp/ With the mouth wide open; in an attitude of wonder, expectation, or eager attention. —
https://www.wordnik.com/words/agape

[6] Beloved of Christ, the Devil is a Liar

Your eyes saw my unformed body; all the days ordained for me were written in your book before one of them came to be.

Psalm 139:16

The devil's plan is to take you out or overwhelm you with the same old and tried strategy. He used the same strategy on Adam and Eve in the beginning. Satan's strategy is to tempt you with the desires or cravings of the flesh like food, drink, or sex. If that doesn't work, then Satan tempts you on the grounds of popularity or stardom. And finally, the devil will test you in the area of power. Every human desires to have power, however, we should not seek power for the sake of it.

When the devil succeeds in his plot, you are left full of shame, guilt, and feeling unaccepted. This creates a sense of purposelessness. It is what Viktor

Frankl[19] referred to as *existential vacuum*, a crisis of meaning, so to speak.

Despite the devil's temptation, we still retain authority on how to respond. Viktor Frankl postulates:

> *The one thing you can't take away from me is the way I choose to respond to what you do to me. The last of one's freedom is to choose one's attitude in any given circumstance.*

Having a sense of being chosen and totally accepted by God correlates to the purpose for which we were created.

---

[19] Viktor Emil Frankl (26 March 1905 – 2 September 1997) was an Austrian psychiatrist and Holocaust survivor, who founded logotherapy, a school of psychotherapy that describes a search for a life's meaning as the central human motivational force. Logotherapy is part of existential and humanistic psychology theories.

[6] Beloved of Christ, the Devil is a Liar

Because you are chosen and accepted by God, you have inherent value. Your identity in Christ comes with intrinsic dignity and integrity. As the bearer of the image of God, your self-worth is part and parcel of your identity. God created each of us with inherent gifts, talents, and abilities that define who we are.

The Bible says:

Look at the birds of the air, they do not sow or reap or store away in barns, and yet your heavenly Father feeds them. Are you not much more valuable than they?

Mathew 6:26

Here Jesus was ascertaining that we tend to worry about material things, which is predicated on a misunderstanding of our value before God. It is important to know and understand how much God loves and cares for us. If God is concerned with feeding birds, how about you? Hence we should comprehend that we are so valuable to God the Father and Jesus Christ our Lord.

Furthermore, Jesus Christ asserted:

> *... Consider the lilies of the field, how they grow: they neither toil nor spin, and yet I say to you that even Solomon in all his glory was not arrayed like one of these. Now if God so clothes the grass of the field, which today is and tomorrow is thrown into the oven, will He not much more clothe you, O you of little faith?*
>
> Mathew 6: 28-30

If God cares about the grass of the field, obviously He is concerned about our wellbeing because we are in the image of God. We are so valuable to God the Father because we are His

[6] Beloved of Christ, the Devil is a Liar

representatives on Earth. We are vice regents and ambassadors of Christ. An ambassador is an official representative of his country in another country. Our original country is the Kingdom of Heaven, and we are tasked by God to bring heavenly culture on Earth.

Apostle Paul gives credence to this:

> *We are therefore Christ's ambassadors, as though God were making His appeal through us. We implore you on Christ's behalf. Be reconciled to God. God made Him who had no sin for us, so that in Him we might become righteous of God.*
>
> *2 Corinthians 5: 19-20*

Paul is attesting that Earth is a foreign country in which we are representative of the King whose throne is in the original country, the Kingdom of Heaven.

To put this in perspective, let's consider an ambassador of the United States of America (USA) in Kenya. While in Kenya, the USA ambassador is the official representative of the President of the USA, so much so that he/she goes by the title of *His/Her Excellency*. The ambassador is the messenger of the official position of his country of origin, he/she speaks what the President desires, not his/her own opinions. Therefore, as ambassadors of Christ we are tasked to do the will of God, not our own will.

The devil works tirelessly to distort this identity. How? By imparting it in people's minds that they are here to do their own bidding. Multitudes spend entire lives running after selfish desires instead of being dedicated to the will of God in their lives.

The devil uses ignorance as his number one tool for misrepresenting facts, but even more importantly, the facts of the Kingdom of God. Satan doesn't want us to have insight and discernment of the gift of salvation. When Paul says, "He who knew no sin became sin for us," Paul implies that we

[6] Beloved of Christ, the Devil is a Liar

switched places with Jesus. Jesus made us righteous through an act of love that required shedding of His blood on the cross. In the process He took on our sin.

What a remarkable and affectionate gift for us from God the Father and Jesus Christ our Lord. Because if God's justice was to be carried out against us, none of us would be in right standing with the Law of God. However, the justice of God is countered by the mercy of God. You are loved by God, and he remembers your sins no more.

The Bible says:

For I will forgive their iniquities and will remember their sins no more.

Hebrews 8:12

Satan wants you to believe that God doesn't care about you, but the devil is the father of lies. Lying is the native language of the devil.

REDISCOVERING IDENTITY

No matter what challenges you encounter in life, just know that you are loved by God. Here are some scriptures that validate God's love for us:

Certainly the faithful love of the Lord hasn't ended; certainly God's compassion isn't through! They are renewed every morning. Great is your faithfulness.

Lamentations 3: 22-23

My lips praise you because your faithful love is better than life itself.

Psalm 63:3

[6] Beloved of Christ, the Devil is a Liar

I give you a new commandment: love each other: Just as I have loved you, so you must also love each other.

John 13:35

Do not be afraid little flock, for your Father has been pleased to give you the kingdom.

Luke 12:32

REDISCOVERING IDENTITY

But you are a chosen people, a royal priesthood, a holy nation, God's special possession, that you may declare the praises of him who called you out of darkness into his wonderful light. Once you were not a people, but now you are the people of God; once you had not received mercy, but now you have received mercy.

1 Peter 2: 9-10

[7]

Jesus Christ as the Flawless & Exemplary Image of God's Nature

Through Jesus we witness the convergence of heaven and earth, as the flawless embodiment of God's essence, and the supreme manifestation of God's image.

— *Unknown*

ALL IT TOOK was three and half years for Jesus Christ to leave an indelible mark on humanity. From time immemorial, mankind has traversed the never-ending journey in discerning the essence of God. This is a tall order for the finite mind, striving to comprehend the infinite God. Questions have risen such as who God is, and what is our relationship or standing with God. In His infinite wisdom, God chose to reveal Himself to mankind through His one and only begotten Son Jesus Christ.

John the Apostle validates that:

The Word became flesh and made His dwelling among us. We have seen His glory, the glory of the one and only Son, who came from the Father, full of grace and truth.

John 1:14

This parallels Exodus 25:8:

[7] Jesus Christ as the Flawless & Exemplary Image of God's Nature

Let them construct a sanctuary for Me, that I may dwell among them.

Exodus 25:8

He came from Heaven to Earth. Holy and pure in Spirit, yet He took on flesh plus the sin of the world. Clearly, John underscores the fact that he carefully observed and analyzed the nature of Jesus Christ. This nature or essence is referred to as *glory*.

I believe John and the other disciples marveled at the essence of Jesus Christ as He went about His daily life fulfilling the scripture as prophesied. His display of boundless love, kindness, compassion, and grace was a class apart. His honesty, obedience, and truthfulness demonstrated over and again throughout the three and half years of His ministry supremely demonstrated the likeness of God. Through Christ Jesus, the Word became flesh and supremely manifested the love, glory, and character of God. Through Jesus, the invisible God became visible to us. It's in Jesus Christ that God the Spirit metamorphoses into the physical to become God incarnate. Jesus becomes the true manifestation of the invisible God to our physical sight. Scripture evidence depicts that every situation that Jesus encountered, He subdued, be it sickness, demons, storms, and even death. I mean each time Jesus met death, death died. It's this display of dominion over circumstances that drew multitudes towards Him.

Remember that man was created for dominion over all the non-human creation. And it is this exercise of dominion that is the desire for every human on the face of Earth.

The ability to exercise authority is at the heart of mankind's essence, nature, and identity.

Where mankind is unable to exercise authority, a sense of hopelessness pervades the very nature of man. But we see Jesus take on the world and bring everything under His feet. He exercised Kingdom of God influence over worldly circumstances. Important to note is that the coming of the Messiah was to return this Kingdom authority back to mankind. Because obviously, mankind lost this authority with the Fall of Adam.

[7] Jesus Christ as the Flawless & Exemplary Image of God's Nature

Therefore, for mankind to be able to exercise Kingdom authority, it's imperative to study Jesus Christ.

Apostle Paul substantiates this:

> *The Son is the radiance of God's glory and the exact representation of His being, sustaining all things by His powerful word.*
>
> *Hebrews 1:3*

Now, no one knows a product better than the manufacturer. Similarly, no one knows the purpose of the product better the manufacturer. Through Jesus Christ God chose to come from heaven to Earth and demonstrate to mankind what it means to be the image of God, what it means to have dominion over circumstances. Being God incarnate Jesus Christ reflected norms and values that define the essence of God. He was the perfect image of God the Father.

John the Apostle gives credence to this:

Phillip said, Lord show us the Father and that will be enough for us. Jesus answered: Don't you know me, Phillip, even after I have been among you such a long time? Anyone who has seen me has seen the Father. How can you say show us the Father?

John 14: 8-9

Here Jesus attests that in Him, God is revealed. So whether it was humility, kindness, love, compassion, authority, to name but a few, Jesus manifests how we as bearers of the image of God should conduct ourselves. And it's through this Christ-like conduct that mankind should emulate and exercise dominion over Earth.

[7] Jesus Christ as the Flawless & Exemplary Image of God's Nature

For instance, humility was a quality that was and is an embodiment of Jesus Christ. For God to stoop low and take on human flesh speaks to one of the ways that Jesus shows us humility.

Says Paul the Apostle:

For God was pleased to have all His fullness dwell in Him.

Colossians 1:19

Irrespective of being fully God, Jesus went about His duties as fully man. Imagine, Christ Jesus humbling himself before John the Baptist to receive baptism. He didn't have to, but the will of God was the guiding light of His life. Throughout scripture, we observe Jesus obediently set His power aside in words and action to the point of submitting to death on our behalf so that we receive redemption. Therefore, only through Jesus are we called to conduct ourselves as bearers of the image of God.

It's through Jesus Christ that we are to mirror God in our day-to-day living.

For our part, we have to emulate Jesus Christ so as to exercise dominion as required by God. We have to be careful so as not to fall prey to the devil's plotting. We have to be on guard against arrogance, aloofness, and self-righteousness. Certainly, not like the Pharisees.

The Bible says:

[7] Jesus Christ as the Flawless & Exemplary Image of God's Nature

> *Then Levi held a great banquet for Jesus at his house, and a large crowd of tax collectors and other were eating with them. But the Pharisees and the teachers of the law who belonged to their sect complained to his disciples, why do you eat and drink with tax collectors and sinners? Jesus answered them, it is not the healthy who need a doctor, but the sick.*
>
> *Luke 5: 29-31*

Despite being pure, holy, and free from sin, Jesus Christ freely mingled with sinners and had compassion for them. Most of the Christians today are just like the Pharisees. The church isolates itself from the world. This has rendered the church ineffective in being role models of what it means to image God in our work.

Truth be told, I have heard Christians decline to work in certain sectors of society because of the presence of sinners. For instance, Christians refuse or turn down jobs in casinos, bars, politics, or night clubs. This is ludicrous and unreasonable. How then can the church effectively fulfill Jesus Christ's call of proclaiming the Kingdom of God message to all nations?

And this gospel of the kingdom will be preached in the whole world as a testimony to all nations, and then the end will come.

Mathew 24:14

Of the 8 billion people on Earth right now, unbelievers outnumber believers. More people are born than born again. There are more Muslims, Hindus, Buddhists, atheists, than Christians in the world, implying the agency called the Church has been ineffective in attracting multitudes to Christ

[7] Jesus Christ as the Flawless & Exemplary Image of God's Nature

Jesus. Salvation is for the world, not just the church. If only the church were to step out of isolation and reach out to the world!

I believe the ineffectiveness of the church is due to the lack of skill among believers to proclaim the Good News of the Kingdom to the world. Jesus corroborates this:

Then saith he unto his disciples, The harvest truly is plenteous, but the labourers are few; Pray ye therefore the Lord of the harvest, that he will send forth labourers into his harvest.

Matthew 9:37-38

It's now 2023 A.D. and the harvest has even become more plentiful, however, authentic teachers of the Gospel are few.

Why?

Because most of us fall into the trap of thinking that being born again constitutes a lifestyle of congregating with believers and isolating oneself from the unbelievers. We become egotistical and egoistic. This is the *holier-than-thou* effect or *self-righteousness*. As a matter of fact, we condemn the *unbelievers*. But we see Jesus as the perfect manifestation of the nature of God, being receptive to sinners and not even condemning them.

For instance, while seated at the well, Jesus engages a Samaritan woman by requesting a drink of water:

> When a Samaritan woman came to draw water, Jesus said to her, "Will you give me a drink?" (His disciples had gone into the town to buy food.)
>
> The Samaritan woman said to him, "You are a Jew and I am a Samaritan woman. How can you ask me for a drink?" (For Jews do not associate with Samaritans.)

[7] Jesus Christ as the Flawless & Exemplary Image of God's Nature

Jesus answered her, "If you knew the gift of God and who it is that asks you for a drink, you would have asked him and he would have given you living water."

"Sir," the woman said, "you have nothing to draw with and the well is deep. Where can you get this living water? Are you greater than our father Jacob, who gave us the well and drank from it himself, as did also his sons and his livestock?"

Jesus answered, "Everyone who drinks this water will be thirsty again, but whoever drinks the water I give them will never thirst. Indeed, the water I give them will become in them a spring of water welling up to eternal life."

The woman said to him, "Sir, give me this water so that I won't get thirsty and have to keep coming here to draw water."

He told her, "Go, call your husband and come back."

"I have no husband," she replied.

Jesus said to her, "You are right when you say you have no husband. The fact is, you have had five husbands, and the man you now have is not your husband. What you have just said is quite true."

"Sir," the woman said, "I can see that you are a prophet. Our ancestors worshiped on this mountain, but you Jews claim that the place where we must worship is in Jerusalem."

"Woman," Jesus replied, "believe me, a time is coming when you will worship the Father neither on this mountain nor in Jerusalem. You Samaritans worship what you do not know; we worship what we do know, for salvation is from the Jews. Yet a time is coming and has now come when the true worshipers will worship the Father in the Spirit and in truth, for

[7] Jesus Christ as the Flawless & Exemplary Image of God's Nature

> they are the kind of worshipers the Father seeks. God is spirit, and his worshipers must worship in the Spirit and in truth."
>
> The woman said, "I know that Messiah" (called Christ) "is coming. When he comes, he will explain everything to us."
>
> Then Jesus declared, "I, the one speaking to you—I am he."
>
> —John 4: 7-26

However, the woman, like most of us, was quick to point out the differences between her and Jesus. First, is it not impossible for this conversation to even be happening? However, Jesus was courteous and respectful. He listened to the woman and the conversation moved from a water request to the number of husbands she had in the past, to the kind of worship ushered in by Jesus Christ.

All the while, Jesus pushed beyond the boundaries of cultural propriety. He disregarded the prejudice that existed between Jews and Samaritans, not forgetting in those days Rabbis were not allowed to speak with women in public, including a wife or daughter. But Jesus set that aside and gave audience to the Samaritan woman.

By the conclusion of conversation, the woman went back to town and drew multitudes from town to come and see Jesus. This was only possible because Jesus Christ was not judgmental, prejudicial, nor did he condemn the woman. Contrast this attitude of Jesus to most of us today, specifically believers. We act like we are the only fish in the ocean, or the only pebble in the beach sands. Instead we are to emulate Jesus Christ, the unparalleled essence of God.

Apostle Paul postulates that:

[7] Jesus Christ as the Flawless & Exemplary Image of God's Nature

> *The son is the image of the invisible God, the first-born over-all creation.*
>
> *Colossians 1:15*

In his book, *The Divine Image*, Ian A. McFarland expounds that:

> "If God is unknowable in essence, then taking flesh cannot change this fact. To the extent that Jesus is confessed to be truly divine, his essence must be every bit as far beyond creaturely comprehension as that of the God he calls Father. In the flesh no less than out of it, God can only be known through the divine attributes. But all this does not mean that God is knowable in creation in a general sense, apart from Christ. On the contrary, Maximus insists that it is only

through the incarnation that it proves possible for God's attributes genuinely to be known, since only the fact of God's taking flesh allows us to ascribe those attributes to their proper subject and thereby avoid idolatry. For a while God's attributes have permeated creation from the beginning, it is only in the light of Christ that they become visible to fallen humankind in their proper relation to the will and work of God."

Hence, Jesus Christ is the authentic representation of the attributes of God the Father.

Jesus Christ embodies forgiveness as one of the divine attributes of the Godhead that exists in three persons. Intuitively, we are called to forgive those who trespass against us, as God forgives our trespasses.

Luke the physician and gospel writer confirms this:

[7] Jesus Christ as the Flawless & Exemplary Image of God's Nature

Forgive us our sins, for we also forgive everyone who sins against us. And lead us not into temptation.

Luke 11:4

On the basis of forgiveness offered by the crucifixion of Jesus Christ, we are restored and reconciled into our original identity. In our original identity we stand in right alignment to God's purpose and will for our lives. And when we do God's will we discover our true and genuine selves. Our calling, so to speak.

Important to note is that through the act of forgiveness, Jesus Christ also manifested self-sacrifice. Through self-sacrifice Christ put aside his authority and power for our sake, and died on the cross for our sins. Jesus Christ always operated with the *others-centered-mindedness*. On our part, we are called from time-to-time to put aside our superior advantage over another so as to accommodate those who are not worthy of merit.

When it comes to imaging God, no one does it better than Jesus Christ. Eight billion and counting, no human mentor before or after Christ ever lived. It's in Christ that the unknowable God can be grasped via the attributes shown by Jesus Christ, God incarnate. Jesus Christ as God incarnate, that is fully God and fully man manifested the norms and values of the Kingdom of Heaven on Earth. He evidenced a culture of Heaven on Earth, which is the ultimate purpose of God the Father, and that is to extend Kingdom of Heaven rulership on to Earth through mankind.

[7] Jesus Christ as the Flawless & Exemplary Image of God's Nature

Then God said, "Let us make mankind in our image, in our likeness, so that they may rule over the fish in the sea and the birds in the sky, over the livestock and all the wild animals, and over all the creatures that move along the ground."

Genesis 1:26

REDISCOVERING IDENTITY

The Interplay Between Culture & Identity

Culture is not just a part of our identity; it is the mirror that reflects the essence of who we are and the lens through which we perceive the world.

— Unknown

ENGLISH ANTHROPOLOGIST EDWARD Burnett Taylor classically defined "culture" as the "complex whole which includes knowledge, belief, art, morals, law, custom, and any other capabilities and habits acquired by man as a member of society." Based on this definition, Taylor clearly postulated that culture is a human phenomenon. Now, the foundation on which human identity is constructed is culture. Culture is front and center in shaping mankind's values, norms, beliefs, language, behaviors, and attitudes. Through culture individuals are able to gain a sense of belonging in respect to a larger group or community. From one generation to another, preservation and continuity of values, norms, traditions, and language is made possible by culture. Individuality is a product of cultural affiliations. It's this individuality that translates into identity.

The *Partition of Africa*[20] is a prime example which illustrates the influence of culture on a people. Instigated by the Berlin Conference of 1884-1885, the borders for most of the African

---

[20] The Partition of Africa began in earnest with the Berlin Conference of 1884-1885, and was the cause of most of Africa's borders today. This conference was called by German Chancellor Bismarck to settle how European countries would claim colonial land in Africa and to avoid a war among European nations over African territory. All the major European States were invited to the conference. Germany, France, Great Britain, Netherlands, Belgium, Portugal, and Spain were all considered to have a future role in the imperial partition of Africa. —https://www.blackpast.org/global-african-history/partition-africa/

states today came into being. The powers that may be behind the Partition of Africa were European kingdoms (countries) that included Germany, Great Britain, France, Spain, Portugal, and Italy. Important to note is that at the time of the partition, these European countries were monarchies—that is, kingdoms or empires.

The outcome of the Partition of Africa was that the people of Africa found themselves in new geographical boundaries and later took on the cultures of these European kingdoms. In some instances families or relatives were separated by these new boundaries premised on the wishes of the European kingdoms. For instance, Angola became a Portuguese colony, Congo-Kinshasa was a Belgian colony, and Zimbabwe was a British colony.

Despite the fact that these countries share borders, the peoples in them were formerly related. However, after the Partition of Africa each country took on a culture that reflected the norms, values, and language of the colonial master's original country. For instance, the official language of Angola became Portuguese because it was the language of the former Kingdom of Portugal which is the present-day Portugal. While the official language of Congo-Kinshasa became French, which is one of the main languages of Belgium. The official language of Zimbabwe became English which is the language of the United Kingdom of Great Britain.

Almost all African countries ended up taking on the cultures of their former colonizers, language being the major indicator of the cultural influence of the former European monarchs on Africa. An important question to ask is how did these countries come to embrace language, values, and norms of their colonizers (the European monarchs)?

In their efforts to exert power and control over the African continent, former European monarchs each appointed an official representative into their colonies. This official representative, called the *governor,* was a citizen of the European monarch. Important to note is that the governor was never appointed from the local populace of the colony. Why? Because he had to be thorough and knowledgeable of the desires and purposes of the king, he would come from Europe.

[8] The Interplay Between Culture & Identity

The governor was tasked with impacting the colony with the norms, values, language, and traditions from the original kingdom. This was in line with the will and purpose of the king from the European monarch, resulting in the adoption of this new culture by the local populace which became their new identity. Later on as the African countries gained independence from their former colonizers the governors returned to their original countries. But to this day glimpses of the values, norms, and languages of these former European monarchs are noticeable throughout Africa.

This parallels the concept of colonization as desired by God, the King of Kings. Colonization is God's idea borne out of His desire to extend the Kingdom of Heaven rulership to the colony of Earth through mankind. Mankind was tasked with the purpose of dominion over Earth. However, this dominion was to be carried out under the guidance of the Spirit of God, just like the governor (earlier mentioned).

The Spirit's original country is the Kingdom of Heaven. Before the Fall Adam was fully under the guidance of the Spirit of God. Intuitively, Adam manifested heavenly values, norms, and language.

It's safe to say that Adam was an embodiment of wisdom and understanding, counsel and might, well-filled with the knowledge of God because he was full of the Holy Spirit. Hence, an authentic bearer of the image of God on Earth, and thriving in Kingdom of Heaven culture on Earth.

Then came the Fall, resulting in the departure of the Spirit of God from mankind. In the process, mankind lost his authentic identity as the image of God as well as falling from rulership or dominion. From then on man's norms, values, language, and culture became compromised as they took on a worldly aspect. Distortion of mankind's identity became inevitable. In any kingdom the identity of the citizens is reflective of the king. No wonder in our fallen state we reflect the attributes of the devil.

John the Apostle corroborates this:

[8] The Interplay Between Culture & Identity

You belong to your father the devil and you want to carry out your father's desires. He was a murderer from the beginning, not holding to the truth for there is no truth in him. When he lies he speaks his native language, for he is a liar and the father of lies.

John 8:44

Let me put this in perspective, in a colony the populace exhibits a culture consistent with values that are reflective of the king or ruler from the original kingdom. In our fallen state, we manifest values like lying, dishonesty, sexual immorality, murder, and drug and alcohol addictions, all which characterize the essence of the devil, resulting in a distorted image of God, hence a flawed identity.

However, when we accept Jesus Christ as our Lord and Savior and submit to His will, then the Spirit of God produces a culture that is reflective of the values, and norms of the Godhead.

Apostle Paul attests that:

But the fruit of the Spirit is love, joy, peace, forbearance, kindness, goodness, faithfulness, gentleness and self-control. Against such things there is no law.

Galatians 5:22-23

Here Paul points out the values that identify a person whose spirit is in communion with the Spirit of God. In "right standing" with the Kingdom of God, so to speak. These attributes differ from the negative attributes resulting in cravings of the flesh earlier mentioned. Man void of the Spirit of God operates on a self-centered agenda most of the time, if not all the time. On the other hand, a man who is under the counsel of the Holy Spirit has an inner grace resulting in a character that is reflective of Jesus Christ's nature. Hence producing a Kingdom of Heaven culture on Earth.

[8] The Interplay Between Culture & Identity

Without the Spirit of God working in you, you can never fully manifest your authentic identity as the image of God. Your relationship with the Holy Spirit is not an option, but a must if you are ever going to become the person God created you to be.

Cephas (meaning stone) attested that:

His Divine power has given us everything we need for a godly life through our knowledge of Him who called us by his own glory and goodness. Through these He has given us His very great and precious promises, so that through them you may participate in the divine nature, having escaped the corruption in the world caused by evil desires.

2 Peter 1:3-4

It's the Divine power that is the source of everything including knowledge, understanding, and wisdom. For some reason man tends to focus on everything else other than the knowledge of God. Mankind has confidence in the wisdom of men instead of God.

However, the Bible says:

There's a way that seems right to man, but in the end it leads to death.

Proverbs 14:12

But when we abide in God, and He in us, we become partakers of His divine nature. We participate in His divinity and exemplify the true sense of being in the image of God as our identity. Additionally, because God is above corruption, then as bearers of the image of God we should stay away from the ungodly lusts of the world, guarding against conforming to the world—that is, be in the world but not of the world.

If you belonged to the world, it would love you as its own. As it is, you do not belong to the world, but I have chosen you out of the world. That is why the world hates you.

John 15:19

Only with the Spirit of God can an environment that fosters values and norms that align one with the Kingdom of Heaven becomes a reality.

Right standing with the Kingdom of Heaven incubates the Kingdom of God within mankind's spirit, resulting in a *Heaven on Earth* culture. For clarity, the Kingdom of Heaven is the territory or place, whereas the Kingdom of God is the influence of the Heaven territory on Earth. The Kingdom of Heaven is a spiritual realm, but very real. And God's

REDISCOVERING IDENTITY

mandate is for mankind to bring Heaven on Earth, dominion over Earth, so to speak.

Through faith in God we become convicted in our spirits and hearts about the existence of God as well His purpose in our lives. Convictions translate into our beliefs, which beliefs produce morals and ethics that constitute our character. It's this character predicated on the Kingdom of God that defines our identity as authentic images of God. Intuitively, a Kingdom of Heaven culture becomes a reality on Earth.

Jesus Christ perfectly manifested the influence of Heaven on Earth during His three-and-half-year ministry on Earth. In his book, *Discover the Hidden You*, Dr. Myles Munroe attests that:

> "If we go to God and say, God, please introduce me to Your people. God will say, Sure. Here is Christ. But we'll say, No. No. No. I want to meet Christ, to which God will reply, Sure. Here's Christ as He shows us the Church. When we want to meet Christ, God will show us the Church. But we can't

[8] The Interplay Between Culture & Identity

> accept this because we think Christ is in Heaven. No, He isn't. Jesus is in Heaven. Christ is sitting in your clothes, living in the body of the believer. Christ is the essence of God—He's God Himself."

Jesus Christ paid the price in full for our redemption, all we have to do is believe and then by the grace of God we become born again in spirit. When you are struggling with the question of, "Who am I?" come to Christ. Coming to Christ is to trust in Him, receive Him, and cling to Him.

You are who God says you are.

[9]

Espousing the Truth of Who God Says You Are

Your true identity is not found in the opinions of others or in the fleeting circumstances of life. It is anchored in the unchanging truth of who God says you are.

— *Unknown*

USUALLY, THE QUESTION that is asked in attempting to answer one's identity is "Who am I?" And the answer from a worldly perspective is predicated on external factors such as reputation, nobility, accomplishments, and appearance, which is far from the truth. I believe the right answer is premised on asking the right question, and that is "*Whose* am I?" Answering this question creates a departure from envisioning oneself based on the ever-changing worldly standards to the lasting truths grounded in the affirmations of God.

When the Word of God becomes the lamp unto our feet which lights our path...

---

*Your word is a lamp for my feet,
a light on my path.*

Psalm 119:105

... a transformation of the mind takes root in us, resulting in self-discovery borne out of our inherent potential.

"Potential" entails the gifts, talents, and unused ability that is in each of us. However, it's important to understand that your potential is unique to you.

[9] Espousing the Truth of Who God Says You Are

Based on this fact, it would be a waste of time trying to be like other people. Unfortunately, multitudes go through life trying to be everything else other than themselves. In this day and age throngs of people associate with brand name products to gain a sense of self-worth.

For instance, Apple products have a cult following the world over and people are caught up in the never-ending upgrade to the latest Apple watch, tablet, or phone. All in the name of feeling important, as well as boosting confidence. But, like the maker of the Apple phone determines its purpose and identity, the purpose and identity of man is predetermined by God our Creator.

To everything God created, there is inherent purpose that in a fundamental way defines the primary nature or essence of a thing. As all human artifacts are made with inherent purpose that defines their identity, similarly God created everything with inherent purpose. And central to this purpose is the potential that precedes it, the manifestation of which is *identity*.

One day as I returned from doing a seven-mile run, something caught my attention in the parking lot as I approached my car. There on the ground close to my car was a bird flapping its wings but couldn't gain flight. No matter how hard it flapped its wings, the poor thing couldn't take flight. Close observation revealed that something had impaired its ability to fly. Then I realized that without the capacity to fly, the bird had lost its primary purpose that defined its identity. I know there are flightless birds, however this kind of bird that lay helpless on the ground was born to fly. The loss of flight fundamentally altered its primary identity.

Parallel to this, God created mankind for the purpose of dominion over Earth on His behalf. And for everything that God calls for, He provides, implying that mankind has inherent potential that makes it possible for him or her to carry out the dominion mandate. This dominion is closely related to the gifts or talents within each person. Hence, authentic dominion is when one excels in their area of gifting for the benefit of others, resulting in the manifestation of our *identity*.

Consequently, failure to harness our inherent potential and purpose as predestined by God compromises one's identity. Of importance is the requirement to be rooted in our source spiritually.

[9] Espousing the Truth of Who God Says You Are

God being our Spiritual source knows everything about us. And who knows a product better than the maker? Similarly, who knows mankind better than God? Your guess is as good as mine.

I can safely say that if you don't believe in who you are, at least believe in who God says you are.

The story of Gideon in scripture illumines my mind. The Bible says:

When the Angel of the Lord appeared to Gideon, He said, The Lord is with you, mighty warrior.

Judges 6:12

"Angel of the Lord" here refers to Jesus Christ, not just a mere angel, because He appeared to Gideon in human form before the incarnation in the New Testament. Here, Jesus Christ takes on the form of humanity but not fully human as in the New

Testament. Before the appearance of the Angel of the Lord, Gideon was privately threshing wheat in a winepress for fear of being noticed by the Midianites (who would come and take it forcefully). To be addressed as a mighty warrior took Gideon by surprise. I believe he turned around to see if there was someone else being addressed by the Angel of the Lord.

Gideon's response confirms his self-doubt. According to the Bible Gideon replied:

[9] Espousing the Truth of Who God Says You Are

Pardon me my Lord, but if the Lord is with us, why has all this happened to us? Where are all his wonders that our ancestors told us about when they said, did not the Lord bring us out of Egypt? But now the Lord has abandoned us and given us into the hand of Midian.

Judges 6:13

Gideon was a simple man going about his routine business of threshing wheat, and didn't believe what the Angel of the Lord said. Basically, his response was that, "All I have heard are these stories about our past glory, which are not relevant at this moment."

As if being called *warrior* wasn't surprising enough to Gideon, the Angel of the Lord proceeded to say:

> *Go in the strength you have and save Israel out of Midian's hand. Am I not sending you?*
>
> Judges 6:14

The Angel of the Lord doesn't grant Gideon any other kind of supernatural strength. Instead, Gideon is instructed to go *in the strength he already has*. The implication is we *already have* the inherent ability to do whatever God calls us to do, it's a lack of faith which is our undoing.

As you may expect Gideon was still shrouded in a cloud of unbelief. The Bible says:

[9] Espousing the Truth of Who God Says You Are

Pardon me my Lord, Gideon replied, but how can I save Israel? My clan is the weakest in Manasseh, and I am the least in my family.

Judges 6:15

Gideon couldn't see beyond what he knew. There's no way he saw himself as the person up to the task of saving Israel. Afterall, he came from the weakest clan in his tribe, and saw himself as insignificant. This Gideon syndrome is a common phenomenon among us. The tendency to focus on our limitations, instead of trusting in the all-powerful God.

I have heard people speak self-defeating statements like "I can't do it" or "I don't have the skills" or "I don't have the confidence to speak up," ad infinitum. No matter your situation or condition, it's important to trust in God, rely on God, and cling to God.

Even with God's promise to be with Gideon on the mission to save Israel from the Midianites, still Gideon was skeptical:

> *...If now I have found favor in your eyes, give me a sign that it is really you talking to me.*
>
> Judges 6:17

My best guess for this request for a sign is because the Angel of the Lord must have appeared to be exactly like a human being to Gideon. No doubt that Gideon's self-confidence was rock-bottom, and that even the Lord's statement of assurance was not enough to fully persuade him, until he saw a sign. Talk about inexhaustible patience on the part of the Angel of the Lord. The world is filled with Gideons who lack a sense of self-worth coupled with a lack of confidence in who they are. However, the good news is that the Lord

[9] Espousing the Truth of Who God Says You Are

God conforms believers to their predestined purposes.

Apostle Paul attests to this:

And we know that in all things God works for the good of those who love him, who have been called according to His purpose. For those God foreknew He also predestined to be conformed to the image of His Son, that He might be the firstborn among many brothers and sisters

Romans 8: 28-29

From this we deduce that God already knows who we are and what we are to become. That is, He already predestined us. We are not here to figure out who we are, we are here to become what God created us to be. Often a time, things may go wrong in life, but even then God will conform us to our pre-determined destination.

Of importance is our cooperation through obedience to the laws of God. The implication is that by the time we show up in the physical, God has already completed us in the spiritual.

For He chose us in Him before the creation of the world to be holy and blameless in His sight. In love He predestined us for adoption to sonship through Jesus Christ, accordance with His pleasure and will.

Ephesians 1: 4-5

To put this in perspective, I will use the United States as an example pertaining to the issue of adoption. Once an adoption is approved under U.S. law, the adopted individual assumes all the rights of a legitimate son or daughter in their new family.

[9] Espousing the Truth of Who God Says You Are

The adopted person becomes *new*, and connections with the old family are null and void. Similarly, once adopted as sons through Jesus Christ into God's family we become new creations.

Apostle Paul is a prime example of true transformation that represents the meaning of "being called by God" and "become who God says you are." Like most people, before his encounter with Jesus Christ, Paul saw himself through the lens of the world. Paul attests that per world standards we define who we are from a fleshly perspective, that is, before we meet Jesus Christ.

REDISCOVERING IDENTITY

> *Though I myself have reasons for such confidence. If someone else thinks they have reasons to put confidence in the flesh, I have more ... of the tribe of Benjamin, a Hebrew of Hebrews, in regard to the law, a Pharisee; as for zeal, persecuting the church; as for righteousness based on the law, faultless. But whatever were gains to me I now consider loss for the sake of Christ.*
>
> Philippians 3: 4-7

Here Paul is telling us that per world standards of his day, he was affluent and belonged to the upper echelon of society. Intuitively, before coming to Jesus Christ, Paul identified himself premised on worldly standards:

- As a Hebrew of Hebrews (pure Jew), he was genetically a descendant of Abraham,

[9] Espousing the Truth of Who God Says You Are

qualifying him as an heir to God's covenant with Abraham.

- As a Pharisee, he was a member of the strictest and affluent experts of the law.
- And he was mentored by non-other than Gamaliel, the Head of Pharisaical studies then.

You can say he had exclusive membership to the Olympic champions of Judaism. Additionally, Paul was a graduate of the University of Tarsus. Like most of us today, we tend to identify ourselves predicated on worldly accomplishment. However, true identity is one's calling based on what the Creator says you are. It's the calling of the Creator.

After the encounter with the Creator, that is Jesus Christ, Paul functioned in his predestined authority and identity.

The Bible says:

REDISCOVERING IDENTITY

The Lord told him, go to the house of Judas on Straight Street and ask for a man from Tarsus named Saul, for he is praying. In a vision he has seen a man named Ananias come and place his hands on him to restore his sight. Lord, Ananias answered, I have heard many reports about this man and all the harm he has done to your holy people in Jerusalem. And has come here with authority from the chief priests to arrest all who call on your name. BUT THE LORD SAID TO ANANIAS, GO! THIS MAN IS MY CHOSEN INSTRUMENT TO PROCLAIM MY NAME TO THE GENTILES AND THEIR KINGS AND TO THE PEOPLE OF ISRAEL.

Acts 9: 11-15

[9] Espousing the Truth of Who God Says You Are

Who knows the essence and purpose of the creation better than the Creator?

The identity of a creation is premised on the purpose that is pre-determined by the Creator. Intuitively, the identity of man is premised on the royal function as pre-determined by God.

> *Then God said, "Let us make mankind in our image, in our likeness, so that they may rule over the fish in the sea and the birds in the sky, over the livestock and all the wild animals, and over all the creatures that move along the ground."*
>
> *Genesis 1: 26*

REDISCOVERING IDENTITY

[10]

Central to True Identity is the Transformation from Slaves to Sons

In the freedom of sonship, we break the chains of slavery that bound us and rise to embrace the inheritance of our divine identity.

— *Unknown*

THE PILGRIMAGE FROM slaves to sonship is a marathon that brings us into light, defining our authentic self as bearers of the *imago Dei*. In essence, it is a process of spiritual growth and maturity grounded in tests, trials, and tribulations. As descendants of Adam, we are born into bondage, that is, slaves to sin. This results in a longing in every human heart to shake off the chains of slavery and embark on a journey that reveals our true identity. Central to this is the deep-rooted transformation of the mind that reveals our true essence. It's an experience which entails salvation, justification, sanctification, and glorification, commandeered by a communion between the Spirit of God and spirit of man.

In our world today, almost everything is available via fast service making the majority of us short on patience or longsuffering[21]. We have come to believe that almost anything can be realized in a short amount of time, including our own transformation. You can think of any human activity such as farming, banking, telecommunications, transportation, or manufacturing, and you will discover each of these activities now takes half the time it used to in the past. For instance, growing a

---

[21] Longsuffering refers to patiently enduring lasting offense or hardship without immediate retaliation or punishment. — https://www.christianity.com/wiki/bible/how-is-long-suffering-a-fruit-of-the-spirit.html

[10] Central to True Identity is the Transformation from Slaves to Sons

2.5-pound chicken in 1925 required sixteen weeks and approximately 12 pounds of feed. Now, a chicken two times greater the size is grown in less than half the time using about 11 pounds of feed. However, when it comes to transformation of the mind, there's no escalator approach. Instead, it calls for a gradual step-by-step approach because mankind is not here to do his or her own will, but the Will of God the Creator.

Prior to doing the will of God—that is, the priority of God for mankind—man has to be validated by God through tests and trials. To put it another way the devil will unleash his operation on you, and how well you hold up validates your faith in God. The testing of faith is a journey into the wilderness.

The Bible says:

> *And immediately the Spirit drove Him into the wilderness.*
>
> *Mark 1:12*

The background to this scripture is that after the baptism of Jesus by John the Baptist, the Spirit of God led Jesus Christ into the wilderness. While in the wilderness the devil unleashed his deceptive ways on Jesus Christ. Unleashing three major tests on Him, but Jesus Christ overcame the devil's plotting.

It is written in scripture that:

[10] Central to True Identity is the Transformation from Slaves to Sons

Jesus returned to Galilee in the power of the Spirit, and news about Him spread through the whole countryside.

Luke 4:14

Now, if Jesus Christ the Son of God was tested, who can be spared? The testing of our faith is part and parcel of spiritual growth. Remember, we are born into bondage because of the universal sin brought about by the rebellion of first man Adam. In bondage the Spirit of God is absent, and there's no communion with the spirit of man. In bondage, man is slave to sin.

To be in bondage is what you call "spiritual oppression" or "captivity." Breaking free from this spiritual captivity requires one to born again. This is not as simple as it sounds because it requires a renewing of one's mind. We have to be like Nicodemus.

The Bible says:

> *Now there was a Pharisee, a man named Nicodemus who was a member of the Jewish ruling council. He came to Jesus at night and said, Rabbi, we know that you are a Teacher who has come from God. For no one could perform the signs you are doing if God were not with Him.*
>
> *John 3: 1-2*

Not wanting to be seen, Nicodemus tiptoed to Jesus Christ at night, out of fear or for some other reason. He belonged to the strictest sect of Judaism, and he was a member of the Jewish ruling council, the Sanhedrin. Obviously, this was a man who was deeply religious for a long time, but was able to see that Jesus Christ was from God. In a way, Nicodemus represents humanity. He confirms the pharisees knew Jesus was from God, but

[10] Central to True Identity is the Transformation from Slaves to Sons

surprisingly, many of them rejected Him, just as so many do in this day and age.

Jesus replied to Nicodemus:

Very truly I tell you, no one can see the Kingdom of God unless they are born again.

John 3:3

It is not about doing good works, it is not about having degrees in theology, and subscription to any religion will not usher you into the Kingdom of God.

Only *being born again* gives us assurance.

To be born again is premised on faith and under the Grace of God. Paul the Apostle attests that we were held hostage under the law before the coming of faith:

> *Before the coming of this faith, we were held in custody under the law, locked up until the faith that was to come would be revealed.*
>
> Galatians 3:23

Here Paul testifies that we were captive under our own sin before we were salvaged by faith. It is through faith in Jesus Christ we become children of God, implying we have a close relationship with God our Father. This close relationship is characterized by trusting in God, relying on God, and clinging to God no matter what.

The Bible says:

[10] Central to True Identity is the Transformation from Slaves to Sons

For you are all sons of God through faith in Christ Jesus. For as many of you as were baptized into Christ have put on Christ.

Galatians 3:27

Looking up to Jesus Christ is the only way we become adopted into sonship of God's family. As sons of God we manifest our predestined authority and identity. In this regard we are in right standing with God. And through right standing with God, the transformation from slaves to sons takes place. The only way to fully manifest our identity and become what God created us to become is by focusing on the Kingdom of God.

Mathew the Apostle put it this way:

REDISCOVERING IDENTITY

> *But seek first His Kingdom and His righteousness, and all these things will be given to you as well.*
>
> Mathew 6:33

Eight billion and counting, each searching for the meaning and purpose of life.

In every human heart is the longing for a sense of control of our circumstances. Intuitively, this shows we *used to be* in charge, because you can't long for something you never had or experienced. This desire to control is so central to human worthiness and somebody-ness, the lack of it yields a sense of worthlessness, thereby highlighting an important truth—that *who we are is positively correlated to our ability to be in charge*. So, in attempt to exert control over our circumstances, everything we do is premised on this fact.

Since the Fall of Adam, man has engaged in several things in an attempt to rediscover his purpose, which is the dominion mandate:

[10] Central to True Identity is the Transformation from Slaves to Sons

- Religion is one of the activities man engages in hoping to rediscover his purpose. Different religions serve as different routes to answer the question of man's search for meaning, but in vain.

- Additionally, various forms of government have been established by man over the years in a bid to answer this search for meaning deeply embedded in man's heart. However, no human form of government has succeeded. Why? Because man is trying to get to revelation and self-discovery without first truly asking, "What is the longing or desire in my heart that keeps me searching?"

When it comes to searching for anything, once you find it, the search is over. Whatever man is searching for is what first man Adam lost. And what first Adam lost, the last Adam restored. Jesus Christ is the last Adam who returned the Kingdom of Heaven rulership on Earth, dominion so to speak, that first Adam forfeited to the devil.

The Bible says:

REDISCOVERING IDENTITY

> *But very truly I tell you, it is for your good that I am going away. Unless I go away, the Advocate will not come to you, but if I go I will send Him to you.*
>
> *John 16:7*

Here Jesus Christ promises to send the Advocate, the wonderful counselor who is the Kingdom of God. The Spirit of God working in us is the Kingdom of God, the influence that restores us to our original authority and identity. Ladies and gentlemen, with the Kingdom of God, which is the Spirit of God working in us, we are able to exercise dominion and regain our sense of purpose.

And Jesus attests that:

[10] Central to True Identity is the Transformation from Slaves to Sons

But when He, the Spirit of truth comes, He will guide you into all truth.

John 16:13

And somewhere I read that the *truth you know shall set you free*.

Important to note is that as the Spirit of God works in us, we are continually being renewed in mind. We experience spiritual growth and maturity as we strive to emulate Jesus Christ. We keep growing in faith as we overcome test after test. With every test, the Lord God ensures we are not overcome by the test itself, but will always provide us a window to be able to withstand.

> *No temptation has overtaken you except what is common to mankind. And God is faithful; he will not let you be tempted beyond what you can bear. But when you are tempted, he will also provide a way out so that you can endure it.*
>
> 1 Corinthians 10:13

As humans we all encounter similar temptations and only through God's strength are we able to overcome them. Often a time, we face the same temptation over and again as the devil tries to wear us out and give in, but God will not let Satan win, if we put our trust in Him.

Where the Spirit of God abides there is freedom. Paul the Apostle asserts that:

[10] Central to True Identity is the Transformation from Slaves to Sons

And we all, who with unveiled faces contemplate the Lord's glory, are being transformed into His image with ever-increasing glory, which comes from the Lord who is Spirit.

2 Corinthians 3:18

The implication by Paul here is that the Holy Spirit is God, like Jesus Christ and God the Father. And with Spirit of God communing with our spirit we are freed from blindness and ignorance into the truth, which is the knowledge of God. Remaining steadfast in the knowledge that God is seated on His throne no matter what the situation is in our life, liberates us into our predestined authority and identity.

Once we turn to God the veil on our faces is removed and through faith in Jesus Christ we become members of God's family—not only members but *children* of God. However, this transformation is only possible through tests and trials that come our way. Trials are God's way of training us in a bid to validate us.

Throughout scripture, you notice whoever was called by God had to be tested before they stepped into their purpose and genuine identity. For instance, Rahab was a prostitute who later became one of the great-grandmothers of Jesus. And remember Moses, a murderer turned deliverer. How about David, the murderer and adulterer who became the great king of Israel?

Therefore, each one of us is redeemable no matter our situation or circumstances. Whatever oppression we are in, God is able to deliver and free us from it. The most important thing is to remain in God and God in us. John the Apostle put it this way:

[10] Central to True Identity is the Transformation from Slaves to Sons

I am the true vine, and my Father is the gardener. He cuts off every branch in me that bears no fruit, while every branch that does bear fruit He prunes so that it will be even.

John 15:1-2

This implies the Holy Spirit continually works on our identity as the image of God in a bid to transform us spiritually. Even when we bear fruit, setbacks or challenges may arise, but they are a kind of pruning with the sole aim of increasing our spiritual maturity. This maturity is perfected in the age to come.

The Bible confirms this:

Dear friends, now we are children of God, and what we will be has not yet been made known. But we know that when Christ appears, we shall be like him, for we shall see Him as He is.

1 John 3:2

Our complete metamorphosis as children of God will be revealed in the life to come. At present it may not be clear to us, but the clue is that we will be like Him, when He is revealed to us.

Conclusion

Just as an artist's masterpiece reflects the essence of its creator, we, as God's masterpieces, reflect His wisdom, creativity, and infinite potential in the world.

— Unknown

I BELIEVE THE greatest tragedy is to live without an understanding of who you are, even more so than to be dead and not know life. In this day and age it's unfortunate that scores of people are suffering from ignorance of who they really are. Countless people identify as *anything but* bearers of the image of God, the *imago Dei*.

For instance, I came across story about a Canadian soccer player who identifies as transgender and non-binary, being hailed as the first of their kind to play in the Women FIFA World Cup. Transgender and non-binary, what is that? So imprecise and nebulous. Not forgetting LGBTQ[22], and now LGBTQIA+[23]. At this rate we will be running out of the entire alphabet in an attempt to figuring out who we really are.

Working as a psychiatric nurse has brought me face-to-face with a great many people whose identities have been eroded by their prevailing situations. And one of my responsibilities was to re-orient these individuals into understanding the difference between *a condition* that affects one, and *the essence* or *being* of one. It was common to hear individuals define their identity by their condition. For instance, "I am bipolar" or "I am

---

[22] LGBT is an initialism that stands for "lesbian, gay, bisexual, and transgender". —Wikipedia

[23] LGBTQIA, abbreviation, lesbian, gay, bisexual, transgender, queer/questioning (one's sexual or gender identity), intersex, and asexual/aromantic/agender —https://www.merriam-webster.com/dictionary/LGBTQIA

Conclusion

schizophrenic." There were common statements of how these individuals in the mental hospital defined themselves.

But even individuals without mental problems tend to undermine their true identity. How? It's common for many people to believe the opinions of others concerning who they are. It's paramount for anyone to believe in their inner voice rather than letting other folks' opinions prevail. Also, as companies invest millions if not billions in advertising their products so as to win the hearts of buyers, shoppers find significance in owning the so-called brand-name products. In other words, people feel more important and identify themselves by, say, the car they drive, cologne they wear, the coffee they drink, the purse they carry, the shoe they wear, ad infinitum.

However, true identity is premised on the discernment of being created in the image of God.

The concept of being bearers of the image of God transcends physical appearance and entails the nature of who we are as well as our purpose. As humans we possess outstanding qualities or attributes that set us apart from all creation. Because we are created in the image of God, **love**,

kindness, and **compassion** should be naturally abiding in us. **Creativity** and **freewill** are profound qualities that are central to who we are as human beings. We have inherent **dignity** and **integrity** because we are God's image.

Additionally, primary to our identity as bearers of the image of God is **the mandate to govern and manage Earth on behalf of the Creator**. To do this calls for gradual and continuous growth spiritually in the way of God.

John the Apostle attests to this:

> *Whoever serves me must follow me, and where I am, my servant also will be. My Father will honor the one who serves me.*
>
> *John 12:26*

To put this in perspective I will allude to a quote by Alexander Maclaren who postulated that:

Conclusion

> *"Think of one Man standing up before all mankind, and coolly and deliberately saying to them, 'I am the realized ideal of human conduct; I am incarnate perfection; and all of you, in all the infinite variety of condition, culture and character, are to take me for your pattern and your guide."*
>
> — *Alexander Maclaren*[24]

In conclusion, the Bible teaches us true human identity lies in our relationship with God and our perseverance though life's trials. Because we were created for a purpose (dominion) that is directly

---

[24] Alexander Maclaren (11 February 1826 – 5 May 1910) was a Scottish Baptist minister... Maclaren was twice president of the Baptist Union of Great Britain, and he was president of the Baptist World Congress in London in 1905. He received honorary degrees in divinity from both Edinburgh and Glasgow Universities. In 1896, the citizens of Manchester had his portrait painted for their art gallery, and the Anglican bishop of Manchester gave the address when the painting was presented. He said that few speakers had exceeded Maclaren "for profundity of thought, logical arrangement, eloquence of appeal, and power over the human heart". — https://en.wikipedia.org/wiki/Alexander_Maclaren

REDISCOVERING IDENTITY

connected to our true identity, it is our responsibility to seek to do His will, to follow His commands, and to lead a life of love and compassion.

As we navigate the ebbs and flows of life, the complications of existence, it's important we always turn to the timeless wisdom of the Bible, finding direction in each of the profound teachings. So, we should remember an important scripture as we move forward:

*Your word is a lamp for my feet,
a light on my path.*

Psalm 119:105

This verse guides and supports us on our journey toward understanding our true identity. The way forward is to be grounded in this important scripture.

Thank you so much, dear reader, for your time here. I am looking forward to hearing about *your*

Conclusion

journey of rediscovering your true identity in the image of God and the fulfillment which comes with that.

Always remember, *you* are the *imago Dei*, you are created in the image of God.

REDISCOVERING IDENTITY

About the Author

25

ROBERT MULINDWA was born and raised in Uganda, the Pearl of Africa. He currently lives in Nashville, Tennessee USA. Robert's writing is predicated on the idea that each person is born for a purpose with potential or hidden capacity to fulfill their reason for existence.

Robert is holder of a Statistics and Math degree in undergraduate studies, as well as a postgraduate

---

[25] *Author Image © Tucker Photography, www.TuckerPhotograhy.com*

degree in Financial Management and Investment. Robert is also a trained and licensed registered nurse (RN).

Created for Success: Finding God's Will, Our Purpose, & True Happiness is his first book, followed by *Rediscovering Identity: You Are the Image of God, as his second.*

To reach Robert about speaking, appearances, quantity discounts on books, and other matters, please visit:

www.RobertMulindwa.com

Thank You

I SINCERELY HOPE you enjoyed *Rediscovering Identity: You Are the Image of God,* as much as I enjoyed writing it, and that this book, like my first, *Created for Success,* helps you achieve a more fulfilling future, and peace and understanding with your true identity in the image of God.

Again, you could have picked any book, but you picked mine, and for that I'm grateful. I hope it added value and quality to your life. If so, it would be really nice if you could share this book with your colleagues, friends, and family. It may help them as well. You might post a review or your thoughts on Amazon, Facebook, Twitter, and/or simply recommend it to someone.

Your feedback and support will help me improve my craft and fill my heart.

Thank you!

You Were Created for Success!

Make sure to read my first book, *Created for Success: Finding God's Will, Our Purpose, & True Happiness.*

Find out more about me and my journey, and read the first three chapters for free by visiting

www.RobertMulindwa.com.

REDISCOVERING IDENTITY

Notes

Preface

- https://education.nationalgeographic.org/resource/theory-evolution
- https://facty.com/network/answers/science/what-is-the-big-bang/10/

Introduction

- https://nypost.com/2021/11/22/black-alien-gets-fingers-sliced-off-to-create-claw/
- https://Enduringword.com/bible-commentary/genesis-1/

Chapter 1

- https://kingjamesbibledictionary.com.
- https://www.livescience.com/63854-stephen-hawking-says-no-god.html.
- J. Richard Middleton, The Liberating Image- The Imago Dei in Genesis 1.

Chapter 2

- https://www.truthaccordingtoscripture.com/commentaries/spe/genesis-1.php

Chapter 4

- Reference: https://www.worldometers.info/world-population.

Chapter 5

- http://www.arvadachristian.org/devotions/2015/8/11/impossible-forgiveness.
- https://bible.org/seriespage/4-fall-man-genesis-31-24.

Chapter 6

- Mans Search For Meaning by Viktor E. Frankl.
- https://arthurcdoyle.wordpress.com/2014/07/31/all-is-discovered-fly-at-once/

Chapter 7

- The Divine Image; Envisioning the Invisible God- Ian A. McFarland.

Notes

Chapter 8

- https://www.britannica.com/topic/culture.
- Discover the Hidden You- The Secret to Living the Good Life, Dr. Myles Munroe.

Chapter 10

- www.farmwithtyson.com/chicken-production-process/

Conclusion

- biblehub.com/commentaries/john/12-26.htm.
- https://people.com/canada-midfielder-quinn-becomes-first-out-transgender-player-at-fifa-world-cup-7565836.